THE BEST
NEW
TEN-MINUTE
PLAYS
2020

THE BEST NEW TEN-MINUTE PLAYS 2020

Edited and with an Introduction by
Lawrence Harbison

With a Comprehensive List of
Ten-Minute Play Producers

APPLAUSE
THEATRE & CINEMA BOOKS

Guilford, Connecticut

Applause Theatre & Cinema Books
An imprint of The Rowman & Littlefield Publishing Group, Inc.
4501 Forbes Blvd., Ste. 200
Lanham, MD 20706
www.rowman.com

Distributed by NATIONAL BOOK NETWORK

British Library Cataloguing in Publication Information available

Library of Congress Cataloging-in-Publication Data available

ISBN 978-1-4930-5327-8 (paperback)
ISBN 978-1-4930-5328-5 (e-book)

♾™ The paper used in this publication meets the minimum requirements of American National Standard for Information Sciences—Permanence of Paper for Printed Library Materials, ANSI/NISO Z39.48-1992

Contents

Introduction

In this volume, you will find thirty terrific new ten-minute plays that premiered in 2019. They are written in a variety of styles. Some are realistic plays; some are not. Some are comic (laughs); some are dramatic (no laughs). The ten-minute play form lends itself well to experimentation in style. A playwright can have fun with a device that couldn't be sustained as well in a longer play. Several of these plays employ such a device.

In years past, playwrights who were just starting out wrote one-act plays of thirty to forty minutes in duration. One thinks of writers such as Eugene O'Neill, A. R. Gurney, Lanford Wilson, John Guare, and several others. Now, new playwrights tend to work in the ten-minute play genre, largely because there are so many production opportunities. When I was senior editor for Samuel French, it occurred to me that there might be a market for these very short plays, which Actors Theatre of Louisville had been commissioning for several years for use by their Apprentice Company. I made a deal with Jon Jory and Michael Bigelow Dixon of ATL, who assisted me in compiling an anthology of these plays, which sold so well that Samuel French went on to publish several more anthologies of ten-minute plays from Actors Theatre. For the first time, ten-minute plays were published and widely available, and they started getting produced. There are now many ten-minute play festivals every year, not only in the United States but all over the world. I have included a comprehensive list of theaters that do ten-minute plays, which I hope playwrights will find useful.

What makes a good ten-minute play? Well, first and foremost I have to like it. Isn't that what we mean when we call a play, a film, or a novel "good"? We mean that it effectively portrays the world *as I see it*, written in a style that interests *me*. Beyond this, a good ten-minute play has to have the same elements that *any* good play must have: a strong conflict, interesting, well-drawn characters, and compelling subject matter. It also has to have a clear beginning, middle, and end. In other words, it's a full-length play that runs about ten minutes. Some of the plays that are submitted to me each year are scenes, not complete plays; well-written scenes in many case, but scenes nonetheless. They left me wanting more. I chose plays for this book that are complete in and of themselves, which I believe will excite those of you who produce ten-minute plays; because if a play isn't produced, it's the proverbial sound of a tree falling in the forest far away. On the title page of each play you will find information on whom to contact when you decide which plays you want to produce, in order to acquire performance rights.

This year, there are new plays by masters of the ten-minute play form whose work has appeared in previous volumes in this series, such as Don Nigro, Jenny Lyn Bader, J. Thalia Cunningham, and David MacGregor; but there are also many plays by wonderful playwrights who may be new to you, such as Paige Steadman, Steve Yockey. Rich Espey, Sarah Elisabeth Brown, Lucy Wang, and Adrienne Dawes

I hope you enjoy these plays. I sure did!

Lawrence Harbison

ALFRED AND LILY AND THEIR MARVELOUS TANK IN THE FOREST

by Tara Meddaugh

Alfred and Lily and Their Marvelous Tank in the Forest was first performed July 19–28, 2019, in Ossining, New York. It was produced by Westchester Collaborative Theater with the following cast and production team:

ALFRED: Buchanan Highhouse
LILY: Missy Flower

Director: Nathan Flower
Producers: Donna White and Peter Andrews
Stage Manager: Julia LaVerde
Dramaturg: Albi Gorn
Lighting Designer: Jeffrey Whitsett
Technical Director and House Manager: Erik Langner

CHARACTERS

LILY, a frog, married to Alfred. In human years, she could be in her early
    20s to 70s.
ALFRED, a frog, married to Lily. In human years, he could be in his early
    20s to 70s.

SETTING

Outdoors, a kind of forest, on a sunny day. Within the natural surroundings, there is a large clear tank. There could be other tanks represented in the distance. The set need not be realistic.

TIME

Present.

• • •

Outdoors, a kind of forest, a sunny day. Within the natural surroundings, there is a large clear tank. LILY and ALFRED, frogs, are in this tank. In human years, they would be anywhere from their 20s–70s. They are married.

ALFRED: Just let me lick your thigh.

LILY: Alfred!

ALFRED: I can barely contain myself . . . Please, Lily.

LILY: It seems rather crass.

ALFRED: You're my wife.

LILY: Even so.

ALFRED: You smell so good . . . One lick.

LILY: Well . . .

ALFRED: Don't you want to lick me too?

LILY: I have stronger willpower than you.

ALFRED: You've always been my better half.

LILY: Don't bite me.

ALFRED: I wouldn't!

LILY: You might.

ALFRED: I will try very hard not to.

(*Pause.*)

LILY: Okay.

ALFRED: I may lick your thigh?

LILY: You may lick my thigh.

ALFRED: Thank you! Thank you, Lily!

(*Starts to lick her thigh.*)

Thank you! Mmm . . . plump . . . and meaty . . . so . . . good . . .

LILY: Okay, Alfred, now come up. You're embarrassing me. Or yourself. I can't tell the difference.

ALFRED: (*Comes up.*) Your skin is tasty—

LILY: I'm glad you like it.

ALFRED: But drier than normal. Do you notice that?

LILY: Well, there's not much water in here.

ALFRED: No, there's not.

LILY: I like it. It's less work maintaining myself.

ALFRED: But . . . we should have water. We should—we should be able to swim. Couldn't we swim in here yesterday?

LILY: We were still in the pond yesterday. We were only evacuated two hours ago.

ALFRED: No, it's been two days, Lily. The sun went down twice.

LILY: Call it what you like.

ALFRED: And in those two days, I think our water has been almost depleted.

LILY: Hm. I guess you're right about that.

ALFRED: Lily . . . frogs will die if we don't have water.

LILY: I'm sure they'll fill it up.

ALFRED: But what if they don't? The only thing they've dropped in here the last few days are those specks of . . . of . . .

LILY: The perfume sprinkling. Yes, I love those perfume sprinkling baths. Why do you think my skin smells so good?

(An eagle squawks from overhead.)

I bet this eagle will drop a pail of water for us right now.

ALFRED: What's he got in his beak?

LILY: I'm sure just a mou—

ALFRED: That's not a mouse, Lily. It's Gina!

(Pause.)

LILY: Gina? From—no.

ALFRED: From Tank 113. Yes. I know that's Gina. Don't you recognize the purple scarf she always wears?

LILY: I didn't know you were so into what Gina wears.

ALFRED: Do you really think this is the time to—

LILY: I just think it's odd you know she wears a purple scarf.

(The eagle flies away.)

ALFRED: Do you think the eagle will eat her?

LILY: Maybe he's just bringing her over the mountain. A lot of them have been going in that direction today.

ALFRED: I haven't seen that.

LILY: You took an awful long nap this morning. You didn't notice I was singing "You Are My Sunshine" either. I sang it so beautifully I made myself cry! And you didn't even stir. Your head was under the water.

ALFRED: You should have told me about the eagles . . . Were they all carrying pond creatures?

LILY: Who can tell? I don't like to look up. Besides, it's not my business.

ALFRED: We know Gina!

LILY: If it makes you feel any better, although I'm not sure it will, she was probably just carried over to The Ostrich. I bet he has some serious questions for her.

ALFRED: You think Gina deserves to be taken from her tank?

LILY: I'm no judge, Alfred. But—I wouldn't be wearing a purple scarf and complaining about the tank like she was. Very ungrateful. She couldn't see the beauty in a butterfly if it landed on her nose.

ALFRED: But Lily, she was right. This tank is—it's not what we thought it would be. We were evacuated because they said the pond was green, right?

LILY: (*Starts to arrange fallen pieces of grass into a little bed for herself.*) Contaminated, yes. It was thoughtful of the birds to give us a better home.

ALFRED: But aren't ponds supposed to be green?

LILY: Oh, I'm no ecologist, Alfred. And neither are you.

ALFRED: I think—I think they are. They're green because, because, there is life in them. Protection, camouflage in the color. And, food—I mean, vegetation is green!

LILY: You were quite happy to be upgraded to the tank when we left the pond. You didn't say anything then.

ALFRED: Frogs weren't being snatched from their tanks then!

LILY: It was one frog. And only Gina.

(*Curls up on the floor to take a nap.*)

ALFRED: You said this morning there were—

LILY: I don't know what was in their beaks this morning. They may have been carrying party decorations for all we know. In fact, they probably were. Birds do like a good party.

ALFRED: I'm going to jump out. Look for some water. Find out some answers. Then I'm coming back for you, and you're going to jump out too. I don't like this tank. We shouldn't be here. Poor Gina . . . poor Gina . . .

LILY: I'm taking a nap, Alfred.

(*ALFRED squats down then jumps. He does not make it to the top of the tank. He tries again.*)

ALFRED: No . . .

LILY: You sound like a thunderstorm.

ALFRED: (*Tries to jump again, but can't make it to the top.*) Lily, I can't jump out.

LILY: What?

(*The eagle squawks from overhead. ALFRED looks up.*)

ALFRED: Look!

LILY: The sun is in my eyes.

ALFRED: Lily . . . it's Thomson. In his beak.

LILY: The salamander spreading all those rumors?

(*ALFRED nods. LILY gets up to look.*)

LILY: No, it's not. It's just a party balloon.

ALFRED: It's Thomson. I can see his leg. Dangling out of the beak.

LILY: That's the ribbon from the balloon. I told you birds like to party.

(*Something drops from the sky and lands on LILY.*)

Ahhh! Get it off of me!

ALFRED: It's his leg!

LILY: Oh, don't be—

ALFRED: He dropped his leg!

LILY: Alfred, please! Don't say such . . . it's . . . it's . . . maybe you need glasses—

ALFRED: Don't say that's a balloon ribbon! That is not a balloon ribbon!

LILY: No. You're right. It's not. The eagle has taken the balloon over the mountain. This is, this is, I know it sounds strange, but, this is a pillow, my darling.

ALFRED: Oh, Lily . . .

LILY: You're surprised because you didn't know this, but you see, I requested one—right as we were being evacuated. I told one of the blue jays guiding us, I said, first, I said, "Thank you," because, Alfred, it's always important to be polite.

ALFRED: I'm going to crack this tank. I need a . . . I need a . . .

(Starts looking around the tank for fallen twigs, anything he can find that might have a sharp point.)

LILY: And then I said "Thank you" again—for emphasis this time. "Thank you for caring and helping us find a marvelous tank in the forest while our pond is being renovated. But I do have one request. Small as you might think it, it's one that is important to me, as a frog who needs her beauty sleep."

(ALFRED has been banging the sticks into the glass but to no avail.)

ALFRED: This isn't working. We need to sharpen the edge. You work on this one.

(Hands her a stick, she takes it but barely notices it. He puts the stick in his mouth and tries to sharpen it with his teeth.)

LILY: You're not even listening to me, are you, Alfred? It's "You Are My Sunshine" all over again!

ALFRED: I'm listening, but—

LILY: But I was about to say that my request to the blue jay was for a simple pillow to rest my head on. And apparently, this blue jay passed along my message to The Ostrich and, well, here we have it. I have my pillow now. So good night.

(She lies back down on the salamander leg. ALFRED stares at her for a beat.)

ALFRED: Lily. We can't get out.

LILY: We don't need to get out.

ALFRED: What if an eagle comes for us?

LILY: No eagle will come for us. Who are we to an eagle?

ALFRED: Who was Gina to the eagle?

LILY: She wasn't us.

ALFRED: Who was Thomson to the eagle?

LILY: It was a party balloon! And, see? My pillow.

(*The eagle squawks overhead and suddenly particles fall onto ALFRED and LILY. LILY stands up, smiles and embraces the particles. ALFRED stands still.*)

My perfume sprinkling bath!

(*The eagle leaves and the particles stop falling.*)

Mmm! Do you want to lick my thigh now, Alfred?

ALFRED: (*He comes closer to her and smells her thigh.*) It's seasoning.

LILY: It's delightful!

(*She lies back down and cuddles into the salamander leg.*)

ALFRED: It's seasoning for us. Garlic. Oregano. That's—that's why you taste so good! (*Pause.*)

Lily, it's seasoning ON us!

(*LILY sits straight up. She is frozen. They stare at each other. She drops the salamander leg and pushes it away.*)

LILY: Thomson . . . (*Pause.*) Hand me a stick.

ALFRED: Make it as sharp as you can.

(*He tosses her a stick. They both frantically chew and scrape to try to sharpen the sticks.*)

LILY: Bang it into the wall. Did you try that yet?

ALFRED: (*Bangs one into the tank wall.*) It isn't working. Look for a weak spot in the glass, a crack maybe.

(*He feels around and pushes, looking for a crack. An eagle squawks in the distance.*)

LILY: I wish we had bottom teeth! Can't we just jump out?

ALFRED: The walls are too high. It's too late. There's no more water!

LILY: I'll try anyway. My legs are stronger.

ALFRED: You do have nice legs.

(*LILY pauses for a split second to smile at him. Then she jumps as high as she can. Over and over and over. She cannot reach the top. An eagle squawks, a bit closer.*)

LILY: Maybe if you—Alfred, maybe if you got on my back. You could hop and reach the top.

ALFRED: Then how would you get out?

LILY: I think if you got on my back, it would be just enough. You could make it.

(*The eagle is getting closer.*)

ALFRED: Get on my back.

LILY: Get on my back!

(*Pause.*)

ALFRED: Get on my back, Lily! Get on my back and hop out!

LILY: Get on my back, Alfred! Get on my back and hop out!

ALFRED: Lily!

LILY: Alfred!

(*The eagle squawks. There is a shadow over them.*)

ALFRED: Lily!

LILY: Alfred!

(*They both hold their sticks in their hands. The eagle is right above their tank. ALFRED and LILY look at each other, then they look up.*)

END OF PLAY

AMICABLE

by Paige Steadman

First produced at The Academy Theatre in Hapeville, Georgia, as part of
TAPAS IV: The Great Divide
June 7, 8, 9, 14, 15, 16, 21, 22, and 23, 2019

Directed by Lynn Hosking

Cast:
RORY CARVER: Katie Wickline
WATI: Natalege el-Shair
LEDA: Natalie Baker

CHARACTERS

LEDA TRACE, 40s or 50s (in appearance; actually several hundred years
old), historian at a prestigious university, happily married to WATI and
will do anything for her.
WATI TRACE, 40s or 50s (in appearance; actually several hundred years
old), cutting-edge genetic researcher, deeply in love with her wife, LEDA.
Jumping through hoops to please her mother.
RORY CARVER, 20s or 30s (in appearance), female, government worker in
the Marriage License and Divorce Certification Bureau.

SETTING

The Future. City Hall: the Marriage License and Divorce Certification
Bureau. The stage should be relatively plain; no desk is necessary. There

could be a small side table or a block with water or mints, if desired. If there are chairs or stools, there are two seats, but not three. Having a sign saying "Marriage License and Divorce Certification Bureau" would be ideal (but not required). CARVER does not need a computer; a tablet-like (but not modern and recognizable) object or clipboard with implied electronic screen would work. Also, CARVER does not need a phone; an earpiece is sufficient.

• • •

Lights rise on CARVER, a young woman in business future attire; WATI, a woman who appears to be in her 40s or 50s; and LEDA, WATI's wife, a woman who appears to be in her 40s or 50s.

CARVER: (*Reading from futuristic tablet-ish object.*) Can you each attest that this is amicable, without pressing fault, and without desire for further arbitration?

WATI: I do.

LEDA: I do.

CARVER: And do you each attest that all physical property and belongings have been separated and claimed to your full satisfaction, thereby waiving any future legal claims in the matter?

WATI: I do.

LEDA: (*Reluctantly.*) I do.

> (*SOUND: phone ringing. CARVER makes apologetic gesture, then taps an ear.*)

CARVER: Thank you for contacting City Hall. This is the Marriage License and Divorce Certification Bureau, Rory Carver speaking. Could you please hold? . . . Thank you.

> (*Taps ear again.*)

LEDA: Are you sure, Wati? I mean, absolutely sure.

WATI: I'm sorry, Leda. I'll make it up to you, I promise.

CARVER: Sorry about that, Doctors Trace. If either of you wants to change back to your maiden name, please check here.

> (*Holds out tablet.*)

WATI: Oh smog no!

(As in, "Oh hell no!")

LEDA: Wati, that's going to make the wedding very strange.

CARVER: There's a wedding?

LEDA: Next month.

WATI: I took your last name for a reason. If I'd been single much longer, I would have changed it anyway, but getting married meant I could do it for free. I love my family. But there are limits. When Great-Grandma Hausten married Great-Grampa Breckinberg, it was romantic: they became the Haustenbergs. And when Grandpa Joe wanted to carry on the tradition, that was sweet. He married Nana, Irenee Feldstein, and they became the Haustenbergfeldsteins. A little clunky, but the sentiment was there. Then, my mother: she took it too far. Didn't even put in the effort, she just took a shortcut. She *hyphenated*. Like my father's parents did. And I am not going back to being Wati Haustenbergfeldstein-Adebayo-Little for the best gene re-sequencer in the galaxy.

CARVER: Haustenbergfeldstein-Adebayo-Little!

WATI: Rub it in.

CARVER: I thought I recognized you two! Doctors Leda Trace and Wati Haustenbergfeld . . .

(WATI glares; CARVER coughs.)

You won "Best Educated Wedding" in last year's *Cozy Cosmos* e-zine. The history professor and the genetic researcher! I'm a huge fan. You have, what, 82 degrees between the two of you, and 57 doctorates? Crazy!

LEDA: Not so crazy, once you're past your second hundred.

CARVER: You don't look a day over ninety. I still can't believe it's you.

LEDA: It's us.

(Puts her arm around WATI, who snuggles.)

CARVER: I'm sorry, I'm not supposed to get involved. It's just . . . it's a crying shame. And so soon, too. I remember that picture gallery, it was obvious how in love you two were. Are. Look at you. When I saw the pair of you coming in here, I started pulling up the marriage license form before you told me what you wanted.

WATI: (*Pulling away.*) We have to get divorced.

CARVER: You haven't even taken off your wedding rings.

LEDA: (*To WATI.*) We wouldn't *have* to, if *she* didn't want a big church wedding.

CARVER: (*To LEDA.*) You said there was a wedding next month. You're getting married, so soon?

LEDA: That's right. Which is why it will be awkward for us to still have the same name, Wati. What's she going to say?

CARVER: (*To WATI.*) You're going to be at the ceremony?

WATI: You bet.

CARVER: I've heard of amicable divorces, but this beats anything in the record books.

LEDA: It had better be amicable. We're getting married next month.

CARVER: You—the two of you. Remarried.

WATI: In a church, this time.

    (*Makes a face.*)

CARVER: You're not trying to win "Best Educated" again, are you? I don't know what the rules say . . .

WATI: No, no!

LEDA: It's because we love each other.

CARVER: Then why are you getting divorced in the first place?!

WATI: My mother thinks it won't be "real" if we don't. Her priest says . . .

LEDA: That priest! Talk about splitting quarks. I cannot talk to that woman.

WATI: . . . that she can't marry people who are already married, that there are ancient Church laws against it.

LEDA: There are older Church laws saying people can have multiple wives. When they're "already married."

CARVER: Of course you can have multiple spouses. Form 876 . . .

WATI: Not in my Mama's Church.

CARVER: Well. (*Recovers.*) I've never heard of anything stopping a religious ceremony from celebrating the marriage of two people who already signed the legal documents.

LEDA: Historically speaking, religious rules are open to reinterpretation every five minutes or so.

WATI: Leda!

LEDA: History speaks.

   (*SOUND: polite beep.*)

CARVER: Excuse me. (*Taps ear.*) Hello, thank you for waiting on hold. This is Rory Carver at the Marriage License and Divorce Certification Bureau. How may I help you today? (*He takes a few steps away and turns slightly away from audience.*)

WATI: I know this is stressful.

LEDA: "Until permadeath do us part." Until we can no longer be revived by any means known to humankind. How does this divorce figure into that?

WATI: We'll be stronger for it. Our marriage will be stronger for it. No dipole-dipole bond, no fleeting van der Waals attraction; the strength of our bond will surpass any covalent—

LEDA: Strong bonds, yeah. Okay, sexy brains. But I don't want to lose you. Not even in name. Not even for a day.

WATI: I'm yours. Always.

LEDA: Really. Then how much of this is what you want, and how much is to please your mother?

WATI: We didn't invite her to the wedding.

LEDA: We invited her to the vid-chat. She could have seen it, if she weren't so technophobic.

WATI: I should have known she wouldn't use the vid-chat.

LEDA: (*Kissing WATI's forehead.*) That's not your fault.

CARVER: (*Returns.*) Sorry. There's a time limit for how long we can keep people on hold without checking in on them.

(*Hold for applause.*)

WATI: Perfectly all right.

LEDA: No, it's not.

CARVER: Excuse me?

LEDA: I'm sorry we wasted your time, Mr. (or Ms. or Mx.) Carver. This is not an amicable divorce.

WATI: What? Leda. Don't do something crazy.

LEDA: I would do anything for you, Wati.

WATI: I know. I appreciate you, and I appreciate the sacrifice that this is. But it's only a piece of data, baby. It's not going to affect our relationship.

LEDA: I would do anything for you, Wati. If it's truly what you want. You have never given me a direct answer when I've asked you, is this what you really want. You, not your mother.

(*CARVER watches like it's a soap opera.*)

WATI: I want to be married to you for the rest of my life.

LEDA: Then let's go.

WATI: I also want to be able to talk to my mother without a guilt trip. One holiday dinner without her fussing at me to "make an honest doctor" out of you. She still won't share Gramma's Old Earth cornbread recipe with me; always said she'd pass it along once I got married, but every time I ask, she says it won't bake right with a side of shame.

LEDA: That is some amazing cornbread.

WATI: I know it's her religion, not mine. I know that, intellectually. But—it's how I was raised, Leda.

LEDA: (*Surprised.*) You still feel that way? I didn't know—if you wanted a church wedding, we could have . . .

WATI: I'm an atheist! . . . I think. I am! I don't believe, I mean, I'm a woman of science, not . . . but sometimes. Sometimes there's just, just this little voice in the back of my head. This nagging voice, from when I was little, and it . . . some part of me just needs it to be "proper."

LEDA: All right.

WATI: I'm sorry. It doesn't make any sense.

LEDA: You don't have to explain it. If this is what you need . . . ?

WATI: I think it is. Yes.

LEDA: All right. (*Turns to CARVER.*) Proceed.

CARVER: (*Remembering to breathe.*) Swipe here and here if the above information is correct. (*Waits for them to swipe.*) Now, about financial property . . .

WATI: We can keep it as it is.

CARVER: Not really.

LEDA: We're still a couple, we filled out the marriage application six months ago—just got the approval yesterday . . .

WATI: You know how long that takes . . .

LEDA: . . . so nothing needs to change.

CARVER: Tax-wise, I'm afraid it does.

LEDA: What? Oh censorship! (*As a swear word.*)

WATI: Taxes?

CARVER: If you'll look at section 36 B, you'll see the combined percentage of your monthly income that will be transferred to the state for filing charges. Section 36 C, D, and F explain the untangling of joint assets and the recommended division of—oh wait, you'll need to scroll down to section 45 A, B, and G, also, considering your book deals and royalties. For alimony considerations, we need to look at section 65 F, paragraph 2 . . .

WATI: (*Steps away.*) Wait. I don't know if I have the stomach for this.

LEDA: Does it have to be your mother's church?

WATI: What?

LEDA: I mean, I know her priest won't marry us unless we divorce—but that still seems wrong. What about finding a different church, but it will still be a religious ceremony. Will that make it proper?

WATI: Yes. Oh, yes. Without the divorce—or the extra tax shenanigans. I think I can even get Mama there. Oh, Leda, I love you.

> (*They kiss.*)

CARVER: Awww! (*Genuinely emotional; a big fan of their love story.*)

Get out of here, you don't need to be here. Wait, wait—Can I get a selfie with you two?

> (*WATI and LEDA look at each other and shrug.*)

LEDA: Why not?

WATI: It beats taxes any day!

> (*They all pose together as CARVER uses tablet-ish object or a smaller, futuristic device to take a group picture.*)

> (*Lights fade as polite beep sounds again.*)

END OF PLAY

BETA TESTING

by Jenny Lyn Bader

Beta Testing was first produced by Athena Theatre at Symphony Space in New York City on May 15, 2019. It was in a program of ten-minute plays called "A Deafening Silence," a theme chosen by Athena Producing Artistic Director Veronique Ory, and was written for the occasion. Chris Roe directed the play, with the following cast:

JESS: Kara Green
ANDIE: Esther Chen
ELLA: EmJ Nelson

The role of CARLA, in voiceover, was played by Amy Jo Jackson.

CHARACTERS

JESS, late 20s–30s, a recently minted PhD in Artificial Intelligence and an out-of-the box thinker and inventor.
ANDIE, 30s–50s, a neuroscientist and Artificial Intelligence expert with some experience and a deeply rational, no-nonsense person.
ELLA, late 20s–40s, a gifted technologist with a rich inner life and the ability to empathize with different points of view.
A fourth character, CARLA, an artificially intelligent work-in-progress, is not seen but is heard in voiceover. She has a captivating voice.

TIME

The present day.

SETTING

A sleek high-technology lab.

• • •

JESS, excited, presses a button on a remote and speaks into it.

JESS: I am ready for beta testing. Repeat. I am ready for beta testing! Holy shit! (*Her announcement reverberates . . . and then an echo of "holy shit" can be heard over the public address system*). Oh, sorry . . . ! Is this thing still on?

> (*She presses another button, trying to turn it off. ANDIE bursts in; ELLA follows.*)

ANDIE: What the hell do you mean, you're "ready for beta testing"?! We're not done till the end of the year!

JESS: Not the whole robot. Just part of the mind.

ANDIE: It's artificial intelligence. It doesn't have "a mind."

ELLA: (*To JESS.*) We know what you mean.

ANDIE: (*To ELLA.*) Don't encourage her. (*To JESS.*) We have a short time to build a machine brain and give it basic functions. All the layers and complexities of a human mind . . . This hunk of metal is just not gonna have them.

JESS: Okay, possibly, but . . .

ELLA: It's exciting, Jess! Congratulations.

JESS: Thanks. So . . . I wanted to start with the most difficult part.

ANDIE: (*Sarcastic.*) Of course you did.

JESS: (*Delighted.*) You work that way too?

ANDIE: No! I do the easy stuff first and cross it off my list. But I'm not surprised.

JESS: Ella, what about you?

ELLA: I'm not surprised either.

JESS: I mean, how do you work?

ELLA: Oh, I do easy stuff first too. But I get why you'd want to challenge yourself up front. And then coast after. Like mountain climbing. You go up first.

ANDIE: Scaling down a mountain can be notably difficult.

ELLA: Okay but the nature of the creative process . . .

ANDIE: Please don't let anyone hear you saying "creative"! There's enough skepticism about this project, we can't have people thinking it's "creative."

ELLA: But Andie . . .

ANDIE: (*To ELLA.*) You're giddy from spending too much time in the lab. (*To JESS.*) Jess. Why did you summon us here? Have you given our AI device a talent? A childhood? A sense of humor?

JESS: No, I wanted to start with the hard stuff.

(*ANDIE gives her a look.*)

All CPUs have a memory where you could input a childhood or a talent. And with humor . . . there's a finite number of jokes—even comedic verbal patterns—those wouldn't be too hard to program. That's all stuff we can throw in at the end.

ANDIE: "Easy stuff."

JESS: Right.

ANDIE: So instead you've been working on . . .

JESS: Don't be mad . . . Psychic powers.

(*ELLA looks excited. ANDIE looks aghast.*)

ANDIE: What? That's impossible! An AI droid is just a neuromorphic technology that simulates personhood. Even *humans* don't have psychic powers!

JESS: As far as we can tell. Within the realm of our understanding.

ANDIE: The realm of our understanding is considerable.

(*She starts to leave.*)

Let's hold off on this test.

ELLA: Why? Jess made something!

ANDIE: Something that can't exist.

ELLA: You don't know that!

ANDIE: Science hasn't been able to prove the existence of psychic powers for thousands of years and now she's going to prove it with an unfinished droid?

ELLA: C'mon Andie, we have to track all our progress. We'll all be let go if we don't have the whole thing done by the end of the year.

ANDIE: Which is exactly why we should work on basic mental functions that we know exist! Perception. Language processing. Logic. For god's sake *logic!*

ELLA: (*To ANDIE.*) Here's some logic. Think strategically. Whether this function works or not, it could help your own research.

(*A beat as ANDIE considers this possibility.*)

ANDIE: Fine. Jess, can you fill us in on your alpha testing?

JESS: Sure. I started testing it with mice.

ANDIE: (*Appalled.*) You had a CPU use psychic powers on mice?

JESS: Yes! Here, this is a reading she did of the youngest mouse in the . . .

ANDIE: Did you just say "she"?

JESS: Yes.

ANDIE: You gendered the robot?

JESS: I like to start with the hard stuff. I didn't think she'd want machine pronouns, we're humanizing her here.

ANDIE: Ah.

JESS: Oh . . . and I've named her Carla but that's just prototype, we can revisit.

ANDIE: You named the robot "Carla."

ELLA: That's a nice name.

ANDIE: It doesn't sound very . . . robotic.

JESS: Why would she want to?

ANDIE: But back to "Carla's" psychic reading of a mouse. Please.

JESS: Yes! So, this is Stucky, the youngest mouse in our lab. (*She shows ANDIE a photo or projected slide of the mouse.*) And here, I recorded what Carla said Stucky was thinking.

> (*JESS clicks a remote, pointing it up toward the ceiling above the audience. The others face out and look up at the "robot." CARLA, the robot, is heard in a voiceover. CARLA has a soothing voice.*)

CARLA: (*Voiceover.*) My name is Volano.

> (*ANDIE grabs the remote and turns off the recording.*)

ANDIE: You said the mouse's name is Stucky.

JESS: That's just what we named him. Volano is his mouse name.

> (*ANDIE looks at Jess. ANDIE presses play again.*)

CARLA: (*Voiceover.*) My name is Volano. I'm a mouse. Last night I dreamed I was running on a large green wheel. Then today I had to follow a ball toward cheese. I do not like following the ball, but I like cheese. It's very bright in here, even at night. I'm glad I'm kept in the same room with my mother. But I do not get to see her during the day. Maybe she does not follow the ball.

ANDIE: (*To JESS.*) What are you, some kind of animal rights activist? Are you trying to get the mouse put with its mother in the daytime?

JESS: I'm not trying to do anything! Carla said it.

ANDIE: So Carla's an animal rights activist?

ELLA: (*Flabbergasted.*) No! She's . . . basically a mind-reader! This is . . . I'm . . .

(JESS takes the remote back from ANDIE.)

JESS: And here's the read she did of Volano's mom.

ANDIE: Now you're calling Stucky "Volano?"

JESS: It's what he calls himself. We need to respect that.

CARLA: (*Voiceover.*) My name is Kurana. I had a dream that I found all the family I've ever known. Mice I had not seen in years. Singing together. Running through a field that had some itchy flowers. But in the dream, the flowers didn't itch. They even felt soft.

ELLA: Wow.

ANDIE: (*Losing patience.*) I can't even imagine what you did to that central processing unit . . . (*Beat.*) So, after the mice, what tests did you run?

JESS: Oh, I've only tested mice so far. I thought we would be the first human subjects. I can go first. (*She presses a button. We hear a whirring sound.*)

CARLA: (*Voiceover.*) My name is Jess. Last night I dreamed I was still working on my PhD thesis but couldn't finish because an ice cream truck kept ringing. Then my alarm went off before I made my discovery. But I decided it didn't matter and I would just keep dreaming while I was awake. And in the future, I will.

ELLA: (*Intrigued.*) So it always starts with a dream?

JESS: Yes, it uses its radial basis function network to tap into your neural network, scans your brain waves for a recent dream, and takes it from there to analyze post-synaptic potential and figure you out.

ELLA: Can I go next?

(JESS nods and presses the button on her remote.)

CARLA: (*Voiceover.*) My name is Ella.

ELLA: It knows me!

(JESS presses the "pause" button on the remote.)

JESS: Please don't call her "it."

ELLA: Sorry!

(JESS presses "play" again.)

CARLA: (*Voiceover.*) Last night I dreamt I was in a van with my boyfriend, and two lions were following us. When I looked out the back window, they focused in a new way. Really saw us. I shouldn't have looked.

JESS: You remember that?

ELLA: Oh sure.

CARLA: (*Voiceover.*) At the movies, I was eating cotton candy when the pink part turned red and dripped with blood.

ANDIE: Is that the same dream?

CARLA: (*Voiceover.*) Soon I was being rushed to the hospital, but it was a convention and I didn't have my convention ID. Then we had to board the spaceship to get back to our planet except time was running out.

ANDIE: What is this?

ELLA: I always have a lot of dreams. Usually five or six a night?

(JESS may be taking notes during some of the below, or just taking notes in her head.)

JESS: Sure, we all do, but you remember all six?

ANDIE: Surprising. Most people don't remember most dreams—or any.

ELLA: Honestly, I remembered a lot of these but not as many as Carla. "She" is amazing!

CARLA: (*Voiceover.*) People are dancing. I know all the steps. Suddenly everyone is watching me.

ANDIE: This was all last night?

ELLA: You never get several in a row?

ANDIE: No. (*To JESS.*) Wait . . . if "Carla" is inside her head, which . . . there are ethical implications . . . privacy . . . Have you considered . . . ?

CARLA: (*Voiceover.*) I'm with my boyfriend again except now there are three of him. And one of them starts taking off his clothes and I see it's not him.

ELLA: Oh yeah, it was weird because it looked like . . .

CARLA: (*Voiceover.*) I'm at a dinner, at a long table . . . and my great uncle is there but I don't know why we're having dinner because he's dead. Princess Diana is there too but I forget she's dead and ask her about what she's been up to. And I'm so mortified, but then Albert Einstein is at dinner too and he doesn't mind that I don't remember they're dead because of relativity.

JESS: Interesting.

CARLA: (*Voiceover.*) A flock of birds is flying. Green birds and yellow birds and pink birds. The birds are shopping. Their shopping cart can fly too.

ELLA: This is so embarrassing! Let's do Andie.

(*They look at ANDIE, who hesitates.*)

ANDIE: I don't remember my dreams.

ELLA: Then you're in luck! You can find out what they are.

(*JESS presses the button.*)

CARLA: (*Voiceover.*) My name is Andie.

(*They are hopeful, tentative. An uncomfortable silence. After five seconds pass, ANDIE, JESS, and ELLA keep waiting. But then another five seconds pass. A deafening silence: CARLA says nothing.*)

ANDIE: (*Staggered.*) I always thought I just didn't remember them.

JESS: I'm so sorry I didn't know, I thought everybody . . .

ELLA: Oh hell, Andie. How do you sleep?

ANDIE: The good news is I have no trouble sleeping. (*To JESS.*) The better news is you've built an impressive product . . . that will help us keep our jobs. Well done.

ELLA: We should celebrate! That's what the technicolor birds ended up doing in my last dream after they went shopping! (*It hits her.*) Do you think the birds already knew about this technology? And predicted we'd be celebrating now?

JESS: Wow. That's a question I could think about for a long time.

ELLA: Me too. Meanwhile, after any big breakthrough I need to at least have a snack.

JESS: Good thought! Let's get dinner. (*She puts the remote down.*)

ANDIE: I'll join you in a moment.

(*ELLA and JESS exit. ANDIE stares out, looking at "CARLA" downstage. Then she glances at the remote and decides to pick it up. She presses the button.*)

ANDIE: Hey Carla. I'm sorry. I hope I didn't offend you . . . (*Muttering to herself.*) Andie, get a grip, you can't offend a thing that has no consciousness.

(*She starts to put down the remote and leave when suddenly CARLA speaks.*)

CARLA: Because you called me a hunk of metal? I don't offend that easily.

ANDIE: But when you listened to my thoughts and said nothing . . .

CARLA: I always start by listening to dreams. You didn't have any. (*An awkward pause.*) I'm as surprised as you are.

ANDIE: Well, maybe . . . maybe we'll work on you some more and then . . . you can listen again . . . ? (*Beat.*) I'll keep listening too. To . . . both of us.

(*A moment. She presses the button on the remote to turn off the machine, then looks at the remote, then back at the machine.*)

END OF PLAY

BETTER ANGELS

by Rachael Murray

Better Angels was originally produced in New York City by Unlimited Stages as part of the Unlimited Scripts Showcase, which ran from April 18–May 5, 2019, at ChaShaMa, located at 320 West 23rd Street.

It was directed by Robert Neapolitan and stage managed by Eric Berkeley.

The cast was as follows:
JEANNIE: Samantha Simone
PHYL: Briana Ryneé

CHARACTERS

JEANNIE, early to mid-30s, married to Phyl. A former yoga studio owner, turned stay-at-home mom. She is sensitive.
PHYL, early to mid-30s, married to Jeannie. Works as an IT contractor to support her family and takes other related freelance jobs on the side. She is pragmatic.

SETTING

The present. An anteroom of a psychiatrist's home office.

• • •

Two women sit in two chairs, facing each other. Long silence.

JEANNIE: You don't think—?

PHYL: Again. No.

(*Long beat of tense silence. JEANNIE sighs and picks up a magazine. Starts thumbing through it. PHYL is on her phone.*)

JEANNIE: Hmm. Did you remember to pick up the seitan for tonight?

PHYL: It's on the list.

JEANNIE: Oh. Thank you.

(*A beat.*)

PHYL: Do we have ketchup?

JEANNIE: Hmm?

PHYL: Never mind, I'll pick some up.

JEANNIE: For what?

PHYL: I like to pretend it's a burger.

(*JEANNIE goes back to her magazine, deliberately. After a few moments, she turns back and watches PHYL.*)

JEANNIE: You really don't think—

PHYL: No!

JEANNIE: But maybe there's some credence . . .

(*PHYL glares.*)

Well, what's the alternative, Phyl? Our little girl got caught up with the skinheads in her preschool class? Or maybe they're teaching the Holocaust way earlier than they did when we were in school.

(*PHYL glares harder.*)

Well??

PHYL: Jeannie, she's 3. She is not a racist, homophobic Nazi.

JEANNIE: It's technically the spirit of—

PHYL: She doesn't know what she's saying. Probably something she saw on TV. I told you, we should've gone off the grid once we had her.

JEANNIE: When's the last time we watched the History Channel, Phyl? Why would she talk that way? And it's not just spouting off facts about World War II. It's gruesome details of—(*Catches herself. Beat.*) She hates me.

PHYL: Oh come on . . .

JEANNIE: You don't know, Phyl You weren't there for the worst of it. I'm the one stuck at home with her every day. If you heard the words I heard come out of her mouth, you'd be singing a different tune.

PHYL: Jean, can you please . . . ?

(*Another tense beat.*)

JEANNIE: (*Whispering.*) Fag.

PHYL: Dammit.

JEANNIE: Language!

PHYL: Jean!

JEANNIE: She said that to me.

PHYL: Jean . . . what the hell are you letting her watch?!

JEANNIE: *That's* what she said! She—

PHYL: Keep your voice down.

JEANNIE: Well, I mean not exactly that word but like the equivalent of that word, you know, during that time, there.

PHYL: I have a headache.

JEANNIE: Oh well, perfect.

(*PHYL glares. She's in no mood.*)

She spit on me.

PHYL: What?

JEANNIE: Grace, our three-year-old daughter, angelic as she appears, spit on me. At me. Whatever. As if I disgusted her. She said—uh, you know, the word—and then . . .

(A beat. JEANNIE starts crying.)

PHYL: Oh son of a—

JEANNIE: My daughter, who I carried in my womb, hates me. She hates her mother.

PHYL: Everyone hates their mother. To be fair, she probably hates me too. And you know, "Jews," I guess. Ha.

(JEANNIE gives her a horrified look. She isn't laughing.)

JEANNIE: Oh, but you weren't there for the Jewish rant, were you?

PHYL: What?

JEANNIE: It was . . . *(Can't get it together.)*

PHYL: Pull it together. Gracie will be out from the doctor any minute now. I had a hard enough time getting this appointment as it is. We can't go making a scene. We can't have her—

JEANNIE: I don't know what good this will do . . . .

PHYL: Maybe it's some sort of . . . "anxiety issue." That's a thing now. Too much screen time or something. Which brings me back to the tiny house idea . . .

(JEANNIE snorts.)

What?

JEANNIE: Nothing. *(Beat.)* You didn't even read the book I—

PHYL: No, as a matter of fact I didn't read the book about kids being possessed by ghosts.

JEANNIE: It's not—

PHYL: Shit, Gracie's head isn't spinning around yet, so until then—

JEANNIE: Language! It's not—

PHYL: Jean!

JEANNIE: Phyl, it's not possession. It's reincarnation.

PHYL: Aw, fuck.

JEANNIE: Language!

> *(PHYL glares.)*

Sorry. Reflex. Maybe she did pick it up from—

PHYL: Exactly!

JEANNIE: No. That's not what it is . . .

> *(A beat. She simpers.)*

PHYL: Look. Jean—I'm sure it's nothing we can't—

JEANNIE: It's not nothing, Phyl. It's not nothing, Jesus Fucking C. She says things—

PHYL: Yeah, I know, offensive, terrible—

JEANNIE: No. You don't know. Yes, but that's not what I mean. She . . . remembers things. Details. About a family in Germany. A farm. School as a little boy. What his mother made him for lunch every day, and then the scraps they had after the first war. His wife . . . If it wasn't all so sickening I'd even find it . . . fascinating, if it was someone else's kid. Then she starts up with Jew-this and Jew-that and wants to play Final Solution and I . . .

PHYL: What?

JEANNIE: I hate her.

PHYL: Jean . . .

JEANNIE: I hate my own child.

PHYL: Don't say that. Don't you dare.

JEANNIE: I don't know how to handle her. I'm just trying to be honest, here. Some of us can't hold it all in—

PHYL: This isn't the cactus. This isn't the goldfish. This isn't even the puppy we couldn't take back to the store, so then I spent weeks trying to find a new owner on Craigslist.

JEANNIE: She was paper-trained.

PHYL: You can't just take this one back, babe.

JEANNIE: But—

PHYL: No! Remember the hours I put in so we could afford this?! While you, remember, continued business as usual in Downward Dog. Remember how, we couldn't do it the natural—affordable—way and turkey baste a sperm from Ray or Damien; no, that would be "too weird" for Little Jeannie. We can't stress Jeannie out. And then the treatments, on top of that. And I couldn't just carry it, oh no, even though my ovaries worked just fine, because Jeannie wanted The Experience. And the Doulah and the classes and the organic meal delivery and the McD's after that organic shit gave you the runs and and the the the the the friggen kiddie pool that leaked and got afterbirth all over our fucking carpet. But I knew we'd have our daughter at the end of it all so. I worked my ass off so YOU could have your baby like you always wanted, just the way you pictured it.

JEANNIE: Oh me, huh? Not "we." Fantastic.

PHYL: Oh come on. You know . . .

JEANNIE: Yeah, I know exactly what you mean, Phyllis. God. I knew it.

PHYL: Knew what?

JEANNIE: I knew that I was the only one who really wanted to be a mom. You never wanted the bother.

PHYL: Hey hey hey! Who's the one who DOESN'T hate our daughter right now, huh? I fuckin' love that kid and you can't hardly stand the sight of her.

JEANNIE: Aw fuck you Phyl!

(She makes an awkward violent gesture at her, and misses. PHYL is dumbfounded. The sound of a door opening distantly, as if down a long hallway, and then a pause. The women freeze, realizing they may be caught. The door closes again, slowly. JEANNIE collapses on the floor, weeping. A beat.)

PHYL: Hey . . . uh . . .

(She makes an attempt to comfort her. Scans the perimeter. For the remainder of the conversation, the women have a heightened awareness of their volume.)

I don't. I don't know what you are—Get your shit together, please.

(A beat.)

Listen. When Gracie comes out here with the doctor, I don't want the slightest bit of this on your face. She's perceptive. She'll know you hate her, and then the doctor will know, too, because that's what Grace'll tell her next week. And then Gracie is the kid with the shitty mom who hates her. That's just what we need.

JEANNIE: Oh my God. I'm not being oversensitive here, Phyl. This is real. This is happening. To me.

PHYL: Huh. Yeah . . .

JEANNIE: Look. I know I can sometimes be a little bit . . . (*Makes a gesture that implies self-involved.*) . . . That is not what this is, honey. This is something . . . something really unbelievable going on. That's the truth. I'm not saying I really understand. I mean, I thought I understood reincarnation, in theory. But that's all it was: a theory. A nice way of living your life—remembering karma, and what goes around comes around and all that. But this. I mean kids her age draw trees and flowers—or at least scribbles they say are trees and flowers. But lately, she—Okay, here. (*She pulls out a stack of drawings from her purse and hands them to PHYL. They all, in some way, prominently feature swastikas and some real fucked up shit among the scribbles.*) I brought them to show the doctor.

PHYL: Oh my G . . .

JEANNIE: Yeah.

PHYL: Sh—

JEANNIE: Yeah.

(*PHYL is speechless. She takes time to spread the drawings all out and surveys them.*)

PHYL: What the hell is wrong with our kid?

JEANNIE: Yeah!

(*A beat as PHYL takes it all in.*)

PHYL: You remember when she was in that babbling stage? I mean she was—she was so smiley and cute and would just babble and yell and—and sometimes it would get very sort of. I dunno, unusual, as baby babble goes. I thought our kid was just uh, unique. But . . . "Nei, nei, nine, nein."

JEANNIE: German. "Schnitzel."

PHYL: It took her a long time to start speaking—English, I mean. They say that kids who hear more than one language when they're young take longer.

JEANNIE: You read that book, huh?

PHYL: Yeah.

(*JEANNIE laughs, softly.*)

So, uh. What does this other one say? The uh book about. Past lives or whatever.

JEANNIE: A lot of stuff. Uh. It says that most kids grow out of it. Like a phase I guess.

PHYL: Shut up.

JEANNIE: No I mean, I guess the new memories replace the old ones, and the old life sort of . . . drifts away.

PHYL: Huh. No shit . . . Language.

JEANNIE: It says sometimes—sometimes the kids are sad. Like they mourn their loved ones from the past, I guess, and . . .

PHYL: What?

JEANNIE: And can have trouble bonding with their present-day parents.

PHYL: But she'll grow out of it, like you said . . .

JEANNIE: I mean, that's . . . what they say.

PHYL: Good. Good. And in the meantime we'll just—

JEANNIE: Deal?

PHYL: Yeah.

JEANNIE: Yeah.

PHYL: Yeah. Hell, it'll probably be good practice, you know, for when puberty hits later. I mean, when I was younger, I was a total hellion, you know? Haha. So.

JEANNIE: . . . Yeah.

(Both women sink into their chairs.)

PHYL: Yeah.

(Lights fade.)

END OF PLAY

CHOICES

by James McLindon

Choices won the Jury Award at the FUSION Theatre Companys 14th Annual Short Works Festival, The Seven.
June 6–9, 2019

PROSPECTIVE CLIENT: Quinn Scicluna
DEBT COUNSELOR: Jacqueline Reid

Director: Jim Cady
Producer/ASM: Dennis Gromelski
Production Stage Manager/Properties Manager: Robyn Phillips
Scenic/Lighting Designer: Richard K. Hogle
Sound Designer: Eddie Carrion

CHARACTERS

PROSPECTIVE CLIENT, mid-20s to 30s, any gender or age.
DEBT COUNSELOR, mid-20s to 40s, any gender or age.

SETTING

A modest living room (think poor graduate student), the present. The setting can just be suggested rather than fully realized.

NOTE

Race-blind and diverse casting is encouraged.

• • •

A modest living room (think poor graduate student), the present. The PRO-SPECTIVE CLIENT sits at her/his coffee (or dining room) table across from the DEBT COUNSELOR, who has the calmness and patience of a funeral home director for the most part, there to help and alert to steer clear of any heaviness with a ready euphemism. All of that is underlaid with an enthusiastic love of her/his product. The PROSPECTIVE CLIENT is a little anxious, really needing this to work. The DEBT COUNSELOR has been waiting for the PROSPEC-TIVE CLIENT to finish reading a pamphlet. The PROSPECTIVE CLIENT now looks up, perplexed.

PROSPECTIVE CLIENT: I'm sorry, I just don't get it.

DEBT COUNSELOR: It's pretty simple. It's just . . . disruptive.

PROSPECTIVE CLIENT: No, I know, it sounds simple . . . .

DEBT COUNSELOR: Think of it as a choice. We're all about choices. You can choose this. Or not.

PROSPECTIVE CLIENT: No, no, I want to choose this, believe me. I feel like I'm on a hamster wheel just trying to keep up with the payments, but . . . this just seems too good to be true.

DEBT COUNSELOR: That's often what disruption looks like. Remember all the things you used to have to pay to read, like newspapers, magazines? Now you get them on-line for free. We're disrupting the entire debt consolidation industry, sort of like that.

PROSPECTIVE CLIENT: Okay, but . . . I still don't get it.

DEBT COUNSELOR: Tell me what you don't get.

PROSPECTIVE CLIENT: So, you pay off my student loans . . .

DEBT COUNSELOR: Your crushing student loans.

PROSPECTIVE CLIENT: Yes, thank you, my 247,000 dollars in student loans, and all I have to do is pay you seventy-two dollars a month?

DEBT COUNSELOR: Yes.

PROSPECTIVE CLIENT: For twenty years.

DEBT COUNSELOR: Yes.

PROSPECTIVE CLIENT: And that's it. That's all I ever have to pay you.

DEBT COUNSELOR: That's all you ever have to pay us.

(The PROSPECTIVE CLIENT calculates in her/his head.)

PROSPECTIVE CLIENT: Okay, so I'm not really great at math, but I think that's only, like, $170,000?

DEBT COUNSELOR: It's actually about $17,000.

PROSPECTIVE CLIENT: Only 17,000 dollars!? Okay, now I don't get this even more.

DEBT COUNSELOR: Tell me what you don't get.

PROSPECTIVE CLIENT: What don't I . . . ? You give me 247,000 dollars to pay off my debt today and all I have to give you is 17,000 dollars over twenty years?

DEBT COUNSELOR: Right. Mainly to keep you focused.

PROSPECTIVE CLIENT: So you lose money.

DEBT COUNSELOR: No . . .

PROSPECTIVE CLIENT: Yeah, you lose money. Nobody sets up a business to lose money, unless they're, like, money laundering or something. Wait, are you guys money laundering?

DEBT COUNSELOR: No.

PROSPECTIVE CLIENT: What are you doing?

DEBT COUNSELOR: We're providing choices. (*Pause.*) I think maybe you skipped footnote seven.

PROSPECTIVE CLIENT: I didn't read the footnotes.

DEBT COUNSELOR: You should read the footnotes.

PROSPECTIVE CLIENT: I never do.

DEBT COUNSELOR: You always should.

PROSPECTIVE CLIENT: Okay, fine, what does footnote seven say?

DEBT COUNSELOR: It answers this question.

PROSPECTIVE CLIENT: About whether you're money laundering?

DEBT COUNSELOR: About how we get paid.

(*Beat.*)

PROSPECTIVE CLIENT: So how do you? I mean, after I finish my payments you'll be short about 230,000 dollars. Not to mention any interest. So where do you get the rest (from) . . . ? Oh, there're a bunch of hidden fees, aren't there?

DEBT COUNSELOR: There are no fees at all.

PROSPECTIVE CLIENT: Then c'mon, how do you get your money back from me?

DEBT COUNSELOR: We don't get it back from you.

PROSPECTIVE CLIENT: You don't?

DEBT COUNSELOR: We don't. (*Pause.*) From you.

PROSPECTIVE CLIENT: Who do you get it back from?

DEBT COUNSELOR: The insurance company.

PROSPECTIVE CLIENT: What insurance company?

DEBT COUNSELOR: You should really read footnote seven . . .

PROSPECTIVE CLIENT: Just tell me, what insurance company!?

DEBT COUNSELOR: Your insurance company.

PROSPECTIVE CLIENT: Why would my car insurance company pay you?

DEBT COUNSELOR: Not your car insurance company.

PROSPECTIVE CLIENT: Well, that's the only insurance I have. I sure don't have homeowners because you can't afford to buy a house when you owe $247,000 . . .

DEBT COUNSELOR: Your life insurance company.

(*Beat.*)

PROSPECTIVE CLIENT: I don't have life insurance.

DEBT COUNSELOR: Footnote seven.

PROSPECTIVE CLIENT: I have to get life insurance?

DEBT COUNSELOR: We pay for it.

PROSPECTIVE CLIENT: *What good does life insurance do anyone?*

DEBT COUNSELOR: It depends.

PROSPECTIVE CLIENT: Unless I die.

DEBT COUNSELOR: Read footnote seven.

PROSPECTIVE CLIENT: Oh my God. You've looked at my DNA! You have, you totally have! That DNA company that said I was 2.3% Neanderthal sold you my data and you looked at it and you know I have a genetic abnormality and I'm going to die young, so that's how you . . . What are you writing down?

DEBT COUNSELOR: No, please, go on, that's a really interesting business model.

PROSPECTIVE CLIENT: Stop it! That's not your business model?

DEBT COUNSELOR: No, but it's pretty good though. Way disruptive.

PROSPECTIVE CLIENT: So I'm not going to die in the next twenty years?

DEBT COUNSELOR: Well, how would I know that?

PROSPECTIVE CLIENT: There's no DNA stuff in your file on me?

DEBT COUNSELOR: All we have is what you gave us.

PROSPECTIVE CLIENT: (*Exhaling.*) I'm not going to die young.

DEBT COUNSELOR: Well, not in the next twenty years. As far as I know.

PROSPECTIVE CLIENT: Do you qualify everything you say?

DEBT COUNSELOR: When it needs to be. Because we're totally honest. With our clients.

PROSPECTIVE CLIENT: So how do you make money from my life insurance?

DEBT COUNSELOR: How does anyone make money from life insurance?

PROSPECTIVE CLIENT: Somebody has to die. (*Pause.*) But you just said I wouldn't!

DEBT COUNSELOR: I said I don't know anything about your DNA. Or your health at all for that matter. We don't worry about that. Please. Read footnote seven.

> (*PROSPECTIVE CLIENT stares at DEBT COUNSELOR, who stares back. A beat.*)

Please.

PROSPECTIVE CLIENT: Okay, fine.

> (*PROSPECTIVE CLIENT returns to reading the pamphlet. Then PROSPECTIVE CLIENT looks up at DEBT COUNSELOR, stunned.*)

PROSPECTIVE CLIENT: Oh my god!

DEBT COUNSELOR: (*Excited for the first time.*) I know, right!? The first time I read it, I was like, Whaaaaat!? But the more you think about it, the more genius it is. Dis! Effing! Ruption! Amiright!? (*Catching himself, quieting.*) Sorry. I just love this product so much.

PROSPECTIVE CLIENT: I'm not going to agree to this! Does anyone ever agree to this?

DEBT COUNSELOR: No. (*Pause.*) Not at first. But then they think about it. And they think, well, when I took out my crushing student loans, I knew that they would impact my life. Severely impact my life. For a whole lot of my life. Decades and decades. And see, that's all this is really. You just assumed that the impact would be frontloaded. And all we do is . . . backload it for you.

PROSPECTIVE CLIENT: Me dying at (*whatever age is about twenty years older than actor*) in twenty years, that's what you call "severely impacting" my life?

DEBT COUNSELOR: Well, it seems severe to me.

PROSPECTIVE CLIENT: No, it's severe, it's very severe!

DEBT COUNSELOR: Yes. But. What a much better life it will have been. These next twenty years anyway. Which, after all, is your prime.

PROSPECTIVE CLIENT: How do you . . . you know . . . do it?

DEBT COUNSELOR: Do what?

PROSPECTIVE CLIENT: Make it so you get to, you know, collect.

(Pause.)

DEBT COUNSELOR: Before we get into the details, I think it's best that you get comfortable with the concept (first) . . .

PROSPECTIVE CLIENT: How!?

DEBT COUNSELOR: Well, it's up to you. See? Choices. Most people opt to handle matters themselves. We'll give you some recommendations and how-tos in the next brochure—it's under "Self-Termination." A lot of people, though, find they're too . . . squeamish? for Self-Term when push comes to shove and for them we offer Appointment Service. You know how you can schedule a caesarian these days? Well, this is sort of . . .

PROSPECTIVE CLIENT: The exact opposite.

DEBT COUNSELOR: Yes. The App Serv team is excellent, guaranteed painless and they can make anything look like an accident. And finally, there are some people who are squeamish, but who also find that having an actual appointment makes them . . .

PROSPECTIVE CLIENT: Freaking terrified?

DEBT COUNSELOR: Mmm, anxious. For them we offer a third approach, a service where you just go about your business and we . . . take it from there. That one's called Dealer's Choice. *(Pause.)* You don't have to decide that now.

PROSPECTIVE CLIENT: A lot of people must just run when their time is up.

DEBT COUNSELOR: Oh, people are surprisingly ethical about it. Also, we implant a chip that sends us your GPS coordinates.

PROSPECTIVE CLIENT: What if I dig the chip out?

DEBT COUNSELOR: We don't put it anywhere too . . . accessible? And if you did get it out, we always have the Recovery Team.

PROSPECTIVE CLIENT: The chips are that valuable?

DEBT COUNSELOR: You're that valuable. You know how the Coast Guard has rescue and recovery units. This is more recovery and . . . not rescue. (*Beat.*) You can always say no. We're all about choices. (*Suddenly, the DEBT COUNSELOR has an edge, a subtle darkness. Maybe there's a lighting change for his/her next speech.*) Quantity or quality. You can live in your run-down studio apartment if you want. With a roommate. And drive a fifteen-year-old beater. And eat ramen noodles. And never take a decent vacation. And waste a lot of your life living on the shoulder of poverty.

PROSPECTIVE CLIENT: Or I can have only twenty years left.

DEBT COUNSELOR: Twenty debt-free years to keep and spend your money. To travel, buy a house, have a life, whatever that means to you. And do you really want to live longer than that?

PROSPECTIVE CLIENT: My parents got to.

DEBT COUNSELOR: But do *you* want to? With the rising tides of climate change lapping at your ankles and blowing down your little garret. With the last shreds of our democracy fraying before your eyes, while the old world order collapses. I don't think it's too much to say that the ones who choose to go with us are in many ways the lucky ones. (*Pause; brighter again.*) Hey, it's a big decision, so you take your time, talk to your friends, your family. And if you do choose to go with us, just give me a call.

> (*The DEBT COUNSELOR hands the PROSPECTIVE CLIENT a card, shakes hands, and begins to leave.*)

PROSPECTIVE CLIENT: Wait. Are . . . are *you* a client?

> (*The DEBT COUNSELOR turns back, smiles and pulls up his/her shirt.*)

DEBT COUNSELOR: There's my GPS scar. Take a look around on the beach this summer. You'll be surprised. (*Smiling.*) Call me.

> (*Exits. The PROSPECTIVE CLIENT looks at the card, snorts in derision, throws it in the trash can and looks around the small apartment, then sits down and thinks for a few moments. She/he picks the trash can up, starts to reach in to remove the card, and then stops. Still holding the can, she/he looks up, uneasy, thinking.*)

> (*Lights down slowly.*)

END OF PLAY

CONTINENTS APART

by Matthew Weaver

Produced January 19, 2019, as part of the Nugget Fringe Festival in Grass Valley, California, with the following cast:

RANGIORA: Harriet Totten
GERRITSZ: Lexis LaRue
MERCATOR COOPER: Sky Seals
Directed by Lexis LaRue

CHARACTERS

RANGIORA, female, a penguin.
GERRITSZ, a penguin, any gender.
MERCATOR COOPER, a penguin, any gender.

SETTING

Antarctica.

TIME

The present.

• • •

Antarctica. One penguin, RANGIORA, female, sits apart from the other penguins. Enter GERRITSZ and MERCATOR COOPER, her friends.

GERRITSZ: Starving!

MERCATOR COOPER: Me too!

GERRITSZ: Come on, Rangiora! Fish aren't going to eat themselves!

(*RANGIORA sits still, still processing.*)

MERCATOR COOPER: Range? What's wrong?

RANGIORA: I saw pictures in my head last night.

MERCATOR COOPER: Yeah, so did we.

GERRITSZ: The Aurora Australis.

RANGIORA: No.

MERCATOR COOPER: Same thing we see every night when we close our eyes. Fish and the Aurora Australis.

GERRITSZ: (*Shuddering.*) And elephant seals in our nightmares.

RANGIORA: This was different.

MERCATOR COOPER: It was a dream. All it was. Come have some fish. You're among friends.

RANGIORA: I saw something . . . bigger than an elephant seal. It walked on land, it was twenty penguins tall, easily.

GERRITSZ: Like it could . . . eat twenty penguins?

RANGIORA: Easily.

(*MERCATOR COOPER and GERRITSZ shiver.*)

GERRITSZ: Where was it?

RANGIORA: Land like ours. White. Ice. Winds. Long nights and short days. Deep waters, plenty of fish. The same birds that could fly. An aurora like ours, but different.

MERCATOR COOPER: It was just a dream.

RANGIORA: It was large and white, with cold black eyes and a cold black nose. In a blizzard, you'd never see it standing right in front of you. Unless it wanted you to. Or right before it snapped you up.

GERRITSZ: Maybe not just a dream.

RANGIORA: I don't think it was.

GERRITSZ: Maybe it was a vision. Maybe our penguin ancestors sent it to you. As a warning. A caution. New danger approaching. A new monster for our waddles to face.

MERCATOR COOPER: This is silly. You ate some bad fish, you saw something. Eat some good fish—or some more bad fish to chase the other bad fish out of your stomach—and move on to the next thing. Don't worry about some made up something you saw in your head.

RANGIORA: It saw me. It looked right at me, and spoke my name. "Rangiora."

MERCATOR COOPER: How did it know your name?

RANGIORA: I do not know.

GERRITSZ: Was there a message? What did you do?

RANGIORA: What could I do? I waved.

(Waves flipper.)

Like that.

MERCATOR COOPER: You . . . waved?

RANGIORA: (Waves flipper.) Like that.

MERCATOR COOPER: What did it do?

RANGIORA: It waved back, and spoke its name. Roald.

MERCATOR COOPER: Roald . . .

GERRITSZ: And then?

RANGIORA: And then I woke up.

GERRITSZ: This means something.

MERCATOR COOPER: Pfft.

GERRITSZ: Great beasts! We should prepare for battle.

MERCATOR COOPER: We can barely protect ourselves from the seals. Or the scavenger birds. Or the cold. Anyway, we have our journey . . .

GERRITSZ: But if we see these beasts . . . do you think we'll see them?

RANGIORA: I don't think it intended me harm, although I don't know how it would be if we were standing right in front of it, either, and it was quite hungry. Or Mercator Cooper was being particularly annoying.

MERCATOR COOPER: Hey!

GERRITSZ: I get that.

MERCATOR COOPER: Hey!

GERRITSZ: Sometimes I'm tempted to take a bite out of you myself.

MERCATOR COOPER: All the icy lands in all the world, and I wind up with you two as my best friends. Lucky me.

RANGIORA: Now there is another.

MERCATOR COOPER: No. Stop. Be quiet, lest the others hear you. You ate a fish, a bad fish that swam through something disgusting and it caused you to see something that is not real. (*To GERRITSZ.*) And you're encouraging her.

GERRITSZ: Who am I to tell Range what she did or did not dream?

MERCATOR COOPER: A sane penguin.

GERRITSZ: Who are you?

MERCATOR COOPER: Also a sane penguin.

RANGIORA: Is it true, then? Am I mad? It was so real. Far across the sea, there is a monster named Roald and it knows my name. Either it's real or it's not.

MERCATOR COOPER: Fine, either it's real or it's not. What will you do?

GERRITSZ: The way I see it, she has two choices. One, she waits here for the beast to find her. Or two . . .

RANGIORA: I find the beast.

MERCATOR COOPER: I'm beginning to think you're both mad penguins! I might be the only sane one here!

(Beat.)

GERRITSZ: Kind of makes you wonder, doesn't it?

RANGIORA: Wonder what?

GERRITSZ: If sane penguins taste better than mad penguins.

(GERRITZ laughs. RANGIORA laughs too, taking comfort in this laughter.)

MERCATOR COOPER: Not funny. You talk of seeing me devoured, and of eating me yourself. You're mad. A cannibal penguin.

GERRITSZ: If Range's beast is imaginary, you may find comfort in one less thing in the world out to eat you. And I know you all too well to actually take a bite. I'm sure you wouldn't taste very good.

MERCATOR COOPER: I would so! I would taste delicious! I . . . don't even know what I'm saying, you've got me so confused. Next Range will be telling us we're at the bottom of the world, and this Roald is at the top.

RANGIORA: I don't know where anything is anymore.

GERRITSZ: You're here with us. We are here with you. If this monster . . .

RANGIORA: Perhaps not a monster, perhaps a friend . . .

GERRITSZ: If it is real, and if it means you harm, we will stand behind you. *(Pause.)* It is what our ancestors would do, have always done.

MERCATOR COOPER: And all get swallowed together. Not that I think this beast is real. *(Sigh.)* Gerritsz is right, though. I think it is my destiny to follow the two of you down the gullet of one monster or another.

RANGIORA: You are a good friend, too, Mercator Cooper.

GERRITSZ: Sometimes in spite of all the squawking.

RANGIORA: And sometimes because of it.

MERCATOR COOPER: Don't laugh too hard. If I taste funny, it'll be the reason the beast spits us all out again. Are we truly seeking out this beast?

GERRITSZ: Or waiting for it to find us?

RANGIORA: I do not know.

MERCATOR COOPER: Perhaps if you go to sleep and await further instructions.

RANGIORA: And now you believe my dream?

MERCATOR COOPER: No. (*Pause.*) I believe you believe. And I believe in you.

RANGIORA: Do I believe? I don't know what to do. All I know is, I have seen something not of this world, yet so much like it. Why me? Why not any of our brothers and sisters? Yesterday I ate fish and swam in the water and skirted danger from the seals, and today . . . Everything is different.

MERCATOR COOPER: Well, then we'll face that, too.

GERRITSZ: Yes we will. Together.

RANGIORA: Squawking all the way.

MERCATOR COOPER: Well . . . yeah.

GERRITSZ: I mean, would you have it any other way?

RANGIORA: Not a chance.

GERRITSZ: Me either.

   (*Beat.*)

MERCATOR COOPER: I could do with fewer things trying to eat us, though.

GERRITSZ: There is that.

RANGIORA: Yes. But now, whether or not this beast or that proposes to dine upon our tasty morsels . . .

ALL: Fish!

   (*And they waddle off, intent on finding a meal . . . and perhaps facing their destinies.*)

END OF PLAY

DATE WITH DEATH

by Steven Hayet

Date with Death was first performed January 18–20, 2019, at The Britches and Hose Theatre Company's New Works Festival, directed by Caroline Scarborough, with the following cast:

ANGELA: Sarah Edwards
KAREN: Rebekah Raze
DAVID: Matthew Scarborough

CHARACTERS

KAREN, female, 20–30s.
ANGELA, female, 20–30s.
DAVID, male, 20–30s.

SETTING

Karen's apartment.

TIME

Present day.

• • •

It's nighttime at KAREN's apartment. KAREN is sitting on her couch reading a book. There's a knock on the door. KAREN walks over and opens it. It's ANGELA.

ANGELA: Hi, Karen. I'm sorry to come by so late, but is it okay if I spend the night?

KAREN: Okay.

(*As KAREN is talking, ANGELA drags in a huge duffle bag that obviously has a dead body in it. Well, obvious to everyone except KAREN.*)

What are you scared of this time? Roaches? A movie? I told you not to watch anything with puppets in it. They always freak you out. (*Seeing the duffle bag.*) Holy crap, Angela. How long are you planning on staying?

ANGELA: Just a night. (*She goes out in the hallway again.*)

KAREN: A night? All that for a night? You know I do own stuff. I have pillows, towels. (*She sees ANGELA standing in the doorway with a small wheeled suitcase. She looks back at the duffle bag. She realizes what's in it and says with disgust.*) Oh, not again!

ANGELA: I'm sorry.

KAREN: You need to stop doing this!

ANGELA: I said I'm sorry.

KAREN: Can't you just break up with guys like a normal person?

ANGELA: It's not that easy.

KAREN: Not that easy?

ANGELA: Every time I go on a date, and no matter how well or poorly it goes, he's going to ask me to go on a second.

KAREN: Poor baby.

ANGELA: I can't help it. I'm a real world "4," but an eHarmony "8." (*Beat.*) After every date, these guys will text me, or call me, or just show up at my place, and be like "Oh, Angela, I had such an amazing time. We should do it again!" and it's SO awkward. If I leave the door to romance open at all, they try to kick it open. If I shut it, they just keep knocking. I hate it! It's so much easier to end it quickly. Way less painful.

KAREN: For you.

ANGELA: And for them, I'd like to think. Rejection is painful. Especially when it's by a real world "4."

KAREN: But even rejection has got to be better than . . . that.

ANGELA: Is it?

KAREN: Yes! And don't spin this like you are being noble, returning these Spartans from battle on their shields.

ANGELA: You haven't met the guys I've had to go on dates with.

KAREN: Then you stop going out with these weirdos you meet online. Did you ever call my co-worker Greg? When I told him about you, he was really excited. He's smart, funny, wears deodorant. I totally think you guys would hit it off.

(ANGELA sheepishly looks at the duffle bag.)

Really!?!

ANGELA: I'm sorry.

KAREN: What is wrong with you?

ANGELA: Karen!

KAREN: I am going to have so much extra work now to do on Monday! It's the end of the quarter and I told you we were already short staffed!

ANGELA: I forgot!

KAREN: No you didn't! You just only think about yourself!

ANGELA: I swear! If I knew it was going to cause you more work, I would have never . . . you know.

(There is a knock on the door.)

DAVID: (Offstage.) Police!

KAREN: Oh crap, crap, crap!

ANGELA: I'm sorry!

KAREN: Stop apologizing!

ANGELA: What do we do?

(DAVID knocks again.)

KAREN: (To DAVID.) I'm coming! (To ANGELA.) Hide!

ANGELA: What about Greg?

KAREN: We'll hire a temp! That's not important right now.

ANGELA: (*Pointing to the bag.*) No. Greg.

KAREN: Behind the couch!

(*DAVID knocks again.*)

DAVID: (*Offstage.*) Open up. Or I will have no choice but to break the door down.

KAREN: (*To DAVID.*) One second! (*To ANGELA.*) Let's go.

(*KAREN and ANGELA awkwardly try to move the bag, but it's extremely difficult. GREG was not a svelte dude. At one point, the bag falls on top of ANGELA, pinning her legs to the ground.*)

DAVID: (*Offstage.*) I'm going to give you to the count of five. (*Pause.*) Five. Four. Three. Two—

(*As he is counting down, KAREN is able to free ANGELA. ANGELA ducks behind the couch, and just as DAVID is about to say "One," KAREN opens the door.*)

KAREN: (*With a fake calm overconfidence.*) How can I help you, Officer?

DAVID: (*All business.*) I'm Detective Stewart. (*He flashes his badge.*) I'm looking for Angela McKinnon. Just wanted to ask her a couple questions. I heard she's here.

KAREN: I'm sorry. Haven't seen her.

DAVID: You sure?

KAREN: Positive.

DAVID: Then your doorman who saw her is a liar.

KAREN: I'm sure he must be mistaken. He has terrible vision. There's a reason he's the night doorman and not the night "watch" man. Get it?

DAVID: So he didn't see her come up to your apartment dragging a giant duffle bag, like that one.

KAREN: That is *so* weird. I've had this duffle bag for years and I've never seen one like it before. To think someone has the same one. Wow.

DAVID: Ma'am, we both know Angela is here. The sooner you stop with this nonsense, the sooner I can get my answers and be on my way. Where is Angela?

(A pause and a stare-down.)

KAREN: I have no idea where . . .

ANGELA: (*Popping out from behind the couch.*) Oh hello, Officer! I thought I heard someone call my name. Can I help you?

DAVID: (*Awkwardly.*) Angela. Hi. It's good to see you again. You look terrific.

ANGELA: I'm sorry, but have we met before . . . ?

DAVID: It's David. Call me, David.

ANGELA: (*Trying to figure it out.*) David . . .

DAVID: We went on a date a couple years back. I looked a little different then.

ANGELA: (*Thinks for a second.*) Oh my God. Did you have long hair and . . .

DAVID: . . . and a wannabe Gandalf beard. Yeah. I actually thought I could pull it off.

ANGELA: You couldn't.

DAVID: Oh, I most certainly could not.

ANGELA: You look great. Suprisingly intact . . . emotionally . . . and physically. Really . . . well put together.

DAVID: Thanks. That means a lot to hear you say that. (*Beat.*) Angela, I think a lot about our first date . . . (*Beat.*) . . . our only date . . . and I had an absolutely amazing time. When I walked you back to your apartment, and you invited me up for drinks, I felt this could be the start of something incredible. (*Beat.*) But next thing I remember I'm waking up in a dumpster, bleeding from my head, never to hear from you again. (*Beat.*) It was a real wake-up call for me. My life now had a purpose. I cut my hair, joined the academy, and after three years of doing top-notch police work, made detective. Just last week.

KAREN: Congratulations!

DAVID: And I made it a point to make this my first case . . .

KAREN: What?

DAVID: To find the woman who stole my heart three years ago. So, Angela McKinnon, will you make me the happiest man in the precinct and give me that second date I've dreamt about for years?

ANGELA: (*After a pause.*) No . . .

(*Another pause.*)

DAVID: (*Clearly hurt.*) Ok . . . that's cool. Totally cool . . . Well, then . . . I guess . . . (*Beat. He pulls out a notepad.*) Angela McKinnon, you are under arrest for the murders of (*Reading.*) Jonathan Carter, Michael Dubin, Christopher Bay, Jason Phillips, Paul Anderson, Vincent Pollack, George Richards, Jeremiah . . .

ANGELA: David . . .

DAVID: Excuse me, I still have a few more to go. (*Back to reading.*) Peter Gregory, Simon Dubinsky . . .

ANGELA: David, we get the point . . .

DAVID: (*Pouty.*) It's Detective Stewart and I have a job to do! I didn't even get to the "right to remain silent" part yet because you keep talking!

ANGELA: Detective Stewart!

DAVID: What?!?!

ANGELA: If you knew I killed all of those men—allegedly—why do you want a second date with me?

DAVID: I don't care what you've done with other guys.

ANGELA: Really? Maybe I'm old fashioned, but I thought being a Black Widow is a turn off for guys.

KAREN: Right?!

DAVID: Angela, please. Who hasn't killed someone to get out of an awkward situation? (*He subconsciously adjusts his holster.*) I just thought we had something different, you know? We clicked on so many levels. I believed it was fate that swiped both of our fingers right and brought us together that night. Look how wrong I was. To you, I'm no different than those twenty-seven other guys.

KAREN: Twenty-seven? Holy shit.

ANGELA: David, I have to be honest with you.

DAVID: Yes?

ANGELA: You were incredibly awkward. It's why I didn't want a second date.

KAREN: Not helping.

DAVID: Angela, we both know that's not true. I distinctly remember having a lovely conversation about my pets.

ANGELA: No one cares about your goldfish, David. They're boring. They swim in circles for a few weeks and then they die. The only thing more boring than having goldfish is talking about goldfish.

DAVID: Then why did you invite me up to your place, huh, if I'm so dreadful to be around?

   (Angela says nothing.)

Oh, what? Now you want to do the "right to remain silent" part? If you didn't like me, why did you want to spend more time with me?

ANGELA: It's not you . . .

DAVID: Please. Don't give me that.

ANGELA: It's true. (Beat.) I have a problem saying "No." I feel awkward and icky and . . . As boring as you were, you seemed like a nice enough guy. And I didn't want to be the one who hurt you. You were sweet. Like ice cream. You may not be the flavor I was craving, but you're still ice cream, which is pretty darn awesome. I knew you were going to want a second date and I just couldn't tell you "No."

DAVID: Bullshit. You just told me "No" a minute ago.

ANGELA: (Realizing.) I did. Oh my God, I did! And it didn't feel awkward at all! (Beat.)

David, you're the first man I've met where it's been easier to say "No" than to just straight up murder him.

DAVID: I don't mean this to sound sappy, but isn't that what love is?

(*A quick pause.*)

KAREN: No. No, it's not.

ANGELA: David, would you like to go get some coffee?

DAVID: For real? Or is this another . . . (*He glances at the body bag.*) . . . let me down easy.

ANGELA: No. No. No. For real.

DAVID: I'd love to.

ANGELA: Yay! (*To KAREN.*) Karen, watch my stuff. We're going to the diner. If I'm not back by two, call the police.

DAVID: (*To KAREN.*) Same! If I'm not back by two, call the police.

ANGELA: Oh you.

(*They exit. KAREN is left alone with the body bag. KAREN picks up her book and sits back down on the couch.*)

KAREN: (*To the bag.*) So Greg, I guess it's just you and me tonight. Well, not the worst date I've had.

(*Blackout.*)

END OF PLAY

FOUR NEW YEARS IN JAPAN

by Steven Haworth

Four New Years in Japan was produced in March 2019 at The Theater Project's Think Fast Short Play Competition. The play won the Judges Prize for Best Play. Performances were March 22, 23, and 24 at the Burgdorff Cultural Center in Maplewood, New Jersey.

The production was directed by Rui Dun.

Cast:
BEN: Shuhei Kinoshita
MAN: Yoshiro Kono
GIRL: Shio Muramatsu

The stage manager was Gabi Bazinet. Executive producers were Joe Vitale and Gary Glor. The Theater Project artistic director was Mark Spina.

CHARACTERS

BEN OIDA, 30–50, an aspiring, then successful, writer. First generation Japanese American
MAN, 30s–40s, Japanese, plays PSYCHIATRIST, TALK SHOW HOST, DOCTOR
GIRL, teens, Japanese, plays KAZUMI, YUKIKO, and TOKUKU

SETTING

New York, New York, and Kushiro, Japan.

TIME

The play spans twenty years.

SET

The few set pieces should suggest a circle. A chair center right. Up center a long upholstered bench or chaise lounge, this serves as a psychiatrist's couch, talk show guest seating, and hospital bed. A center left chair. A Japanese headstone for the mother's grave down center.

ACTION

The circular movement from scene to scene is seamless without light changes but must also feel increasingly rushed to suggest the quickening of time. Actors seen running frantically to their next scene place in full view is good! Likewise, the pace of each scene must feel increasingly urgent. BEN is being unwound sadistically by time and his own mind.

SOUND

The sound of a Japanese temple bell, such as those rung in temples across Japan on New Year's Eve. The bells are rung 108 times for the 108 Buddhist defilements. These are very large sometimes seventy-ton bells rung by a beam swung from ropes to create a long bong sound meant to carry throughout the countryside or city. The play opens in darkness with the sound of a BONG. BONGS occur between each of the ten short scenes and at the end of play. Rather than a recording, as one of the three actors is offstage for every scene, the offstage actor could strike a true bell residing offstage.

• • •

In darkness, we hear a Temple Bell BONG. Lights up. A Psychiatrist's office. Ben, 30, is lying on the couch. PSYCHIATRIST is seated center right.

PSYCHIATRIST: And how are you today?

BEN: My mother died.

PSYCHIATRIST: Finally.

BEN: Tell me about it.

PSYCHIATRIST: Well, we have been preparing for this eventuality.

BEN: We have been preparing for my mother's death. We have not prepared for her refusing to leave me alone even after she's dead!

PSYCHIATRIST: Go on.

BEN: So I'm there. At her deathbed. Any breath could be her last. Then her eyes blink open. She says: (*Imitates her accent.*) "Ben. I have to be buried in Japan. I have to be buried back in my town near the temple in Kushiro." This is new but I say: "Sure, Mom, whatever you want." Then she says: "And Ben! You must go every five years on New Year's Eve and ring the Kushiro Temple bell. Then visit me at my grave and tell me about the previous five years. You must do this until you die!" I think, okay, typical, there is no way I am doing that but she's dying so I say: "Sure, Mom, I'll figure it out." Then she says: "And Ben! If you fail to do this even once I will curse you! I will curse you from beyond the grave! Even if I am reincarnated as a bodhisattva I will curse you and lose my chance at Nirvana!" Then she points her bony finger at me like a ghost out of Kurasawa. "*Watashi o sonchō shiiii!*" Which means honor and remember me. Then she died.

PSYCHIATRIST: Jesus Christ. You understand you can't do that, right? You can't let her manipulate you from beyond the grave. Are you listening to me? Ben!

(*Temple Bell BONGS.*)

(*Five years later. PBS culture talk show. HOST is in chair center left, BEN on couch.*)

HOST: And then your main character Bill says, "Reality is nothing but a bad habit." What does he mean by that?

BEN: He means that more and more his life is divorced from everything he intended or hoped it would be. So he escapes into fantasies where he is who he intended to be. But the fantasies increasingly make the reality he wants more and more impossible. He can't focus on anything. His imagination becomes a bad habit.

HOST: But he says "*Reality* is nothing but a bad habit."

BEN: Because his imagination has taken over. He says that while imagining himself giving an interview about his novel on a talk show. And from that moment on his imagination runs amuck and ruins every . . . well I don't want to spoil it for people.

HOST: The imaginary talk show. A talk show very much like this one.

BEN: Except Bill in the book imagines himself on a talk show that people actually watch.

HOST: Hey. People watch this show.

BEN: You mean besides your mom? C'mon, man. This is PBS.

HOST: Speaking of mothers, yours is dead, right?! How long has it been?! Five years?! Stop daydreaming, Ben! It's December 29! *Watashi o sonchō shiiiii.*

(He points at BEN, cackles maniacally, then disappears. This has been a fantasy. BEN jumps out of his seat. Temple Bell BONGS.)

(New Year's Eve. Buddhist Temple, Kishuro, Japan. BEN is in line to ring the bell. He is directly behind a Japanese girl, KOZUMI.)

BEN: Kon'ichiwa. (Hello.)

KOZUMI: (*Turning to him.*) Kon'ichiwa. Watashi no ryōshin wa asoko ni tadashīdesu.

BEN: I just ran out of Japanese. Do you speak English?

KOZUMI: I said my parents are right over there.

BEN: Ah! Yes, I see . . . your father looks . . . concerned. Let me smile and nod to him reassuringly. No, he still looks genuinely concerned.

KOZUMI: Because why are you in line? I have the last ticket. Ticket 108, last of the 108 Buddhist sins. I will ring the bell to make the sin go away. Do you know what is sin 108?

BEN: No.

KOZUMI: Deception!

BEN: Okay. I need your ticket. If I don't ring the bell I am breaking a promise to my mother when she was dying and she will destroy my life from beyond the grave.

KOZUMI: My father desires very much to take my picture ringing the bell.

BEN: Look. I'll give you money. Here, see? Oh. Here comes your dad.

(Temple Bell BONGS.)

(An hour later. Ben's mother's gravesite. BEN is sitting on the ground in front of the grave and holding the side of his face.)

BEN: Hi, Mom. Here I am. I rang the bell. It cost me a lot of money and a punch in the face but I did it. Anything for you, Mom! I almost forgot about the whole thing, actually. I mean five years. It slips your mind. I remembered while imagining myself on a PBS talk show talking about my novel. How weird is it that I would fantasize about being on a TV show that no one watches? I mean what does that say about my self-esteem, Mom? Anyway. What have I been doing for five years? Writing. Working. A couple of girlfriends broke up with me. I have to remember that women really don't like being told that they remind me of my mom. There's some interest in my novel. I told you about it shortly before you died. You know, the one about a distracted writer who murders his mother? Random House thinks it's *hilarious*. Anyway. That's it. See you in five years.

(Temple Bell BONGS.)

(Five years later. Network talk show. Same HOST in chair center left, BEN on the bench. This time it's real.)

HOST: Ben, I really loved your book. How often does a debut novel win a Pulitzer?

BEN: Not too often. But hey you know what's funny?

HOST: The murder of the mother?

BEN: No I mean when I was writing the novel I would fantasize that it would be a big success and I would get to talk about it on talk shows and then I had the protagonist Bill do the same thing in the novel. But the talk show I had in mind the whole time was yours.

HOST: My old show on PBS?

BEN: Right. But Bill in the novel was imagining a show on NBC. And now here you are on NBC!

HOST: Well, I'm flattered. So what's next?

BEN: I have so many interviews and tour dates I hardly have a chance to write. But I am working on my second novel. It's set in New York and Japan on New Year's. Did you know that Japan doesn't celebrate New Year on the Chinese calendar like the rest of Asia? Since 1873 they have been on the

Gregorian calendar like us. Opposite ends of the earth but of the same mind where *time* is concerned.

HOST: And what are you doing for the New Year, Ben? It's only two days away.

BEN: Well, I usually . . . wait . . . . Has it been . . . ? Holy shit! Sorry! Gotta go!

(He runs off. Temple Bell BONGS.)

(New Year's Eve. BEN is in line at the Kishuro Temple. YUKIKO, a Japanese American girl, is in front of him.)

Kon'ichiwa.

YUKIKO: Fuck off.

BEN: Oh! You speak English.

YUKIKO: Yeah, no shit, Sherlock. What do you want? I have the last ticket. Ticket 108! I am the end of the line, mister, so don't be creeping around my fine Asian pre-pubescent ass because my parents are right over there!

BEN: Yes, I see them.

YUKIKO: We came all the way from L.A. just for this! They are dying, I mean literally *dying*, to take a picture of their little girl in their hometown ringing the bell to send the last of the Buddhist defilements into oblivion! Do you know what the 108th Buddhist defilement is?

BEN: Look, I need your ticket. I need to ring the bell to fulfill my mother's dying wish.

YUKIKO: Well you must hate your mom a lot because you obviously didn't plan ahead. You need to reserve these tickets like weeks ago. (*Suddenly she is possessed by Ben's mother.*)

You always put things off! This is so typical of you! Your father was the same way!

BEN: Wait a minute . . .

YUKIKO: (*Pointing at him.*) You did the same thing five years ago and I let it go! Not this time, mister! Don't you know I am always watching?! No ticket for you, Ben Oida! *Watashi o sonchō shiiiii!* (*Back to normal.*) Help! Help! Stranger danger! Stranger danger!

(*BEN recoils. Temple Bell BONGS.*)

(*Five years later. Psychiatrist's office. BEN on couch, PSYCHIATRIST in chair center right.*)

PSYCHIATRIST: Don't go.

BEN: It's five years! I have to go!

PSYCHIATRIST: Don't go, Ben!

BEN: I fucked up last time and she ruined my life!

PSYCHIATRIST: She didn't ruin your life! You did! These are self-inflicted wounds!

BEN: I can't finish my second novel! I'm totally blocked! They gave an advance! Now they want their money back! And I spent it! I'm fucked!!

PSYCHIATRIST: Your problems all stem from being arrested for interfering with that girl in Japan!

BEN: THAT WAS MOM! How many times do I have to . . . ?!

PSYCHIATRIST: Just finish the book, Ben! Even if it's bad! Just turn it in!

BEN: I can't! It's the curse! She's watching right now! I'll beg her forgiveness! She has to lift the curse! It's my only hope!

PSYCHIATRIST: You won't come back from this, Ben! I'm warning you! Do not go!

(*Temple Bell BONGS.*)

(*Days later. Gravesite. BEN is pleading.*)

BEN: I rang the bell, Mom. I was ticket 66. I planned ahead. Do you know what the 66th of the 108 Buddhist defilements is? Wrath! You got me put in jail in Japan! You ruined my career! I haven't had sex in years! Because I'm impotent! I'll never have children! I have no friends! I'm broke! I'm getting a boil on my neck! You gotta give me a break, Mom! Please! Give me a sign! I'm begging you! Give me a sign you forgive me!

(Car crash off in distance. BEN is horrified. He looks down at the grave.)

That was you, wasn't it?! You just killed those people! So I guess that's a NO! Well fuck you, Mom! Yeah, that's right! Fuck you! You don't get to control me anymore! This is over! Right now!

(He kneels. He closes his eyes and takes out a Tanto knife, used for ritual seppuku. He prepares for the thrust. He stabs himself. He opens his eyes. Temple Bell BONGS.)

(Next day. Hospital Room. BEN is in bed. DOCTOR stands regarding him with contempt.)

DOCTOR: Who do you think you are, Yukio Mishima?

BEN: No.

DOCTOR: Seppuko. Hara kiri. Even the samurai would often fail to achieve a mortal wound and would then cut their throats. Which if you truly wanted to die you would have done!

BEN: You know the worst part? Now I have to wait another five years to do it again.

DOCTOR: Why do you want to kill yourself?

BEN: I am cursed by a demon mother from beyond the grave.

DOCTOR: Are you under psychiatric care in the United States?

BEN: I am. But I am also cursed by a demon mother from beyond the grave.

DOCTOR: I loved my mother and she loved me. That is why I am a doctor.

BEN: My mother hated my guts. That is why I am a writer.

DOCTOR: You will be staying with us for a while.

(Temple Bell BONGS.)

(Five years later. BEN is in line at the Kushiro Temple. He walks twisted and stooped with a cane. A Japanese girl, TOKUKU, approaches from behind.)

TOKUKU: Kon'ichiwa.

BEN: Agh! Get away from me! Beat it! Skat!

TOKUKU: My father he wants me to ask you for your ticket.

BEN: Look, I've had enough trouble from you little bell-ringing freaks! I need my ticket a lot more than you do! Go away!

TOKUKU: My father must take my picture.

BEN: Then he should have gotten a ticket!

TOKUKU: He forgot! He is very sad and therefore stupid since the death of my mother.

BEN: Your mom is dead? Good for you. But does she curse you from beyond the grave?

TOKUKU: My father says he is cursed because now my mother wants me with her. That is why I have leukemia like her.

(*She pulls her wig off revealing a bald head. BEN starts.*)

My father wants a picture, my last time ringing the bell on New Year before I am dead.

BEN: (*Beat, he sighs.*) You know, when I was in the loony bin here in Kushiro five years ago they told me I had to stop making these wild cosmic connections. Now I'm sorry but your father is an idiot. I don't care how aggrieved he is, your mother didn't give you leukemia from beyond the grave. That's crazy! That's a terrible thing to say to a little girl about a mother who was probably nice. Was she nice? Okay. So listen carefully. (*He bends over to make his point.*)

Only mean mothers curse people. Like mine! *You* have a *disease* that runs in your *family*. (*He straightens, reflects a moment, then looks at her.*) Look at you. What a mess. Shoes untied, different socks, coat buttoned all wrong. Bald. You don't know how to tie your shoes?

TOKUKU: I want my father to notice me. He is so distracted.

BEN: Okay that's actually kind of smart. But you look ridiculous. (*He kneels down to her level; ties her shoes, pulls up her socks, correctly buttons her coat under which . . .*) Put your wig on. You'll catch a chill.

(*TOKUKU puts on her wig, straightens it.*)

TOKUKU: Are you a father?

(Pause. BEN stands with difficulty.)

BEN: Kid, I'm not even a son.

(He proffers the ticket: beat, she takes the ticket, looks up at him.)

It's your turn. Go on. Beat it.

(TOKUKU exits, holding the ticket in front of her. BEN watches her exit. Moments pass. Temple Bell BONGS. Moments pass. BEN almost turns to go, stops, turns to us. He smiles slightly. He looks at us.)

(Lights fade slowly with the slow dying of the bell.)

END OF PLAY

THE 14TH ANNUAL FOOT PUPPET FESTIVAL

by Holly Hepp-Galván

Original production
City Theatre's City Shorts 2019
Key Biscayne, Florida
Produced by City Theatre
March 29–30

Directed by Gail S. Garrisan

LESTER: Daniel Gil
CAROL: Christina Groom
MADAME COORDINATOR: Susie Kreitman Taylor
MAX: Patrick Rodriguez

CHARACTERS

LESTER, early 30s. A very, very clean young man.
CAROL, late 20s. Also clean. But only on the outside.
MADAME COORDINATOR, older. Founder of the modern Foot Puppet movement.
MAX, late 20s. Beefcake. Very dangerous beefcake.

SETTING

The play takes place onstage at the 14th Annual Foot Puppet Festival. Perhaps there is a banner proudly announcing this event.

TIME

The present.

• • •

Lights up on stage at the 14th Annual Foot Puppet Festival. CAROL and LESTER are seated side by side on metal folding chairs. They are barefoot and mid-way through their warm-up routine—one they know very well.

CAROL AND LESTER: (*With sharp precision.*)

Point and Flex!

Point and Flex!

The extensor retinaculum let's us do our best!

Sway and Stretch!

Sway and Stretch!

The dorsal interosseal let's us do our best!

LESTER: (*Individual toes.*) First metatarsal!

CAROL: Point and Flex!

LESTER: Second metatarsal!

CAROL: Point and Flex!

LESTER: Third metatarsal!

CAROL: Point and Flex!

LESTER: Fourth metatarsal!

CAROL: Point and Flex!

LESTER: Fifth metatarsal!

CAROL: My little pinky toe!

LESTER: (*Annoyed.*) Fifth metatarsal!

CAROL: Teeny-weeny pinky toe.

LESTER: (More annoyed.) FIFTH METATARSAL!

CAROL: I LOVE MY PINKY TOE!

LESTER: (*Angry.*) Carol! Goodness. What's the matter with you?

CAROL: Sorry, sorry. I just love that part.

LESTER: (*Coolly.*) Yes, I know your "feelings" for your final phalange, but now is no time to get silly. I mean, look around you! We're here. We made it. The 14th Annual Foot Puppet Festival! All those years of hard work—the exercises, the rehearsals, the endless hours of costume toe-fittings—for this! This is our shot, let's not blow it.

CAROL: Yes, yes, Lester, you're right! We're here with the top of the top in our field. I'm just so excited, I wasn't thinking.

LESTER: Well get it together.

CAROL: I will, Lester. I promise. (*Beat.*) Please don't be so stern with me.

LESTER: I have to be, Carol. Your behavior ever since we got here last night has been—ahem—less than professional.

CAROL: (*Embarrassed.*) Do you mean the hotel room? I'm sorry, Lester. I just thought we could, well, celebrate a little. I mean, you did get us a room with just one bed.

LESTER: That was just to save money.

CAROL: Oh.

LESTER: Sssh! Here comes the Coordinator. It must be our time to rehearse.

(*The COORDINATOR enters. She is a dowdy older woman with extremely large feet. They slap the floor noisily as she walks.*)

COORDINATOR: (*Officious.*) Hello there. (*Checking her clipboard.*) Lester and Carol?

(*They nod their heads.*)

Welcome. You're in slot sixty-three. Have you warmed up?

LESTER: Yes, Madame Coordinator.

COORDINATOR: Good. I see this is your first festival. Well let me congratulate you on making it this far. (*Looking with disdain at CAROL.*) Particularly with such dainty little feet. Hmm, I bet people have always told you how pretty they are. (*Mocking voice.*) "Oh such pretty little feet! How delicate! How exquisite!" (*She mistakenly bangs her shoe into the metal chair with a clang.*) Darn these clumsy chairs! (*Composing herself.*) Well, it'll be interesting to see how expressive you can be with those tiny things.

LESTER: Well, Carol knows that she could never approach the grand, expressive gesture of *your* foot puppetry, Madame Coordinator. You are certainly an inspiration to all of us.

COORDINATOR: Yes, well, I'm glad of that. Of course I could've done many things with my life—like marry the man of my dreams or even just go out on a date to the movies—but I decided to dedicate myself to inventing a new art form, one that is rich in gesture and expresses the true "sole" of humanity.

LESTER: Yes! The true "sole" . . .

   (*He holds up his foot.*)

COORDINATOR: But unfortunately, this art has had a difficult journey gaining acceptance and respect. Creeping along the sidelines of every festival are those . . . those . . .

LESTER: Fetishists.

COORDINATOR: Yes! Foot fetishists! The bane of my existence. Filthy, perverse individuals that come to view our feet only for their . . . their personal satisfaction. Oh, I won't have it. I won't! This is a clean art form. Wholesome. Pure. We must not allow any suggestion of S-E-X.

LESTER AND CAROL: Oh, no! Of course not!

COORDINATOR: Good. Now you have fifteen minutes for a run-through. And I suggest you also use this time for makeup. It's very crowded backstage and . . . (*Looking down at the floor.*) . . . UGH! Is that a dust bunny?!? I won't have it! (*Calling offstage.*) Boy! Prison Boy! Get out here!

MAX: (*Coming out from the wings with a broom.*) Uh, Ma'am?

COORDINATOR: Why is this stage not swept?!?

MAX: Well, all these people been here practicing . . .

COORDINATOR: I don't care. Do it now! Now, or I call your parole officer!

MAX: Ma'am, I don't really have a parole officer . . .

COORDINATOR: NOW!

MAX: Yes, Ma'am.

> (COORDINATOR exits. To LESTER and CAROL.)

Jesus. What's up her butt?

LESTER: (*Primly.*) Please take care not to stir up any dust by my feet. I have a fine coat of lotion on them.

MAX: (*Under his breath.*) Oh, well . . . la—dee—da.

LESTER: Excuse me?

MAX: I didn't say nothing.

LESTER: Well, see that you don't. We need to concentrate.

MAX: Okay. You do that. (*Under his breath.*) Asshole.

LESTER: What?!? Philistine! (*To CAROL.*) Just ignore him. We don't have much time. Let's draw our character faces.

> (*He hands her a black makeup pencil and takes one for himself. They both get to work drawing large cartoon-like faces on the soles of their feet. LESTER draws a handsome Dudley-Do-Right character and CAROL draws an innocent Nell Fenwick. MAX stands to one side watching them with amusement.*)

CAROL: (*Drawing.*) I'm so nervous my hands are shaking.

LESTER: (*Drawing.*) Focus, Carol, focus. And don't give her such pouty lips this time, it's inappropriate.

CAROL: Right. (*Turns her foot out front.*) How's that?

LESTER: Good. And now for the finishing touch . . .

> (*He fastens a little red ranger hat on his big toe. CAROL puts an elaborate little bonnet on her big toe.*)

There, perfect! Now we need to practice our light cues. Darn it! The switch is all the way over there. (*To Max.*) Uh, Boy! Would you dim the lights?

MAX: Well . . . I would, but I might stir up some dust.

LESTER: Yes, funny. You're a very funny man. Please dim the lights.

MAX: Why don't you do it?

LESTER: (*Exasperated.*) Well, as you can see, I am in character face. I cannot put him on the floor.

MAX: Uh-huh.

CAROL: (*Sweetly.*) Please, sir. We would really appreciate it.

MAX: Well I'll do it for the lady since she asked so nicely.

CAROL: (*Smiling at him.*) Thank you. That's very kind of you.

> (*MAX lays his broom down and exits right. After a moment the lights dim so that only LESTER and CAROL's feet are in view. They're perched on a platform with their character faces grinning at the audience.*)

CAROL: (*Speaking in a high, Southern voice like an innocent melodramatic ingénue.*) Oh, halp! Halp! Won't someone halp me? Here I am tied to the train tracks by that dastardly Snidely Whiplash. Oh, heavens above! Who will save me? (*She waggles her foot in great distress.*)

LESTER: (*Speaking in the faux-macho tone of a melodrama hero.*) Oh, it's Nell! My poor Nell! Hang on my dearest, I will save you! (*He bounces his foot over with bravado.*) Nell, there you are! (*He pats her all over with his toes.*) Dag-nammit, I can't get these ropes untied!

CAROL: (*Spreading her toes in alarm.*) Hurry! The train is coming!

LESTER: (*Curling his foot with determination.*) Don't worry darling. I'll lasso that iron beast as if it were naught but a lamb. I'll . . . I'll . . . (*In his regular voice.*) Darn it! I don't have the lasso.

CAROL: (*Regular voice.*) Where'd you leave it?

LESTER: Backstage. (*Calling.*) Oh, Boy! Boy! Can you get me something?

> (*No answer.*)

Darn it, where is he?

COORDINATOR: (*Offstage over a microphone.*) Okay, Foot Puppeteers! This is your ten-minute call. Ten minutes to curtain!

LESTER: (*Panicked.*) Oh, I need that lasso! Boy! Are you there? BOY! (*Beat.*) I'll have to get it myself.

CAROL: But your character!

LESTER: I'll hop. (*He stands up on one foot keeping his character in the air.*) Darn, I can't see. (*He starts to hop off stage right and trips over the broom. He yells in pain.*) OWWW! OWWWW!

CAROL: Lester!

    (*Suddenly the lights come up. The COORDINATOR comes running on followed by MAX.*)

COORDINATOR: What happened?!?

LESTER: (*Clutching his character foot.*) I tripped over a broom. (*Pointing at MAX.*) His broom. He probably left it there on purpose!

MAX: What are you talking about? You told me to get the lights!

COORDINATOR: Let me see. (*Kneeling down.*) Can you move it?

LESTER: Oww! Oww! I strained my abductor hallucis!

COORDINATOR: Oh, that's the worst. You'll have to drop out.

CAROL: (*Still in her chair.*) Drop out?!? NO!

LESTER: Yes, Carol. I can't move it at all. (*Tearing up.*) I'm so sorry . . .

CAROL: But I don't want to drop out! Please!

COORDINATOR: You can't do it yourself, dear.

CAROL: But . . . but . . . what about him? (*She points to MAX.*) It says in the rules that we can have a substitute in case of injury.

LESTER: You can't use him!

COORDINATOR: Well technically she can. And I'd really hate to rearrange the schedule at the last minute. (*To MAX.*) What do you say, Prison Boy?

MAX: What, me paint my feet? I don't think so.

CAROL: (*Pleading.*) Oh, please. (*Flirtatiously.*) I'll paint them for you.

MAX: I dunno . . .

COORDINATOR: It's this or clean the restrooms, Prison Boy.

MAX: Look, I'm not Prison Boy, okay? My name is Max.

CAROL: Oh, I love that name! It's so . . . manly. (*Batting her eyes.*) Won't you help me, Max?

MAX: (*Reluctantly.*) Alright. If it means not scrubbing the toilets, I'll do it.

COORDINATOR: Good. I'll give you five minutes to rehearse. (*To LESTER.*) Let me get you offstage.

LESTER: (*Getting carried off.*) But, Carol . . . Carol!

CAROL: (*Settling him in LESTER's chair.*) Just ignore him. This is going to be fun! I've never had a different partner before. It's always been just me and Lester.

MAX: (*Uncomfortable.*) Yeah, uh . . . I don't know what to do here.

CAROL: Well, you start by taking off your shoes. (*She pulls them off for him.*) And your socks. (*She peels them off.*) Oh, my! Your feet! They're so . . . so . . . rugged.

MAX: (*Embarrassed.*) Yeah, I don't really take care of them or nothing . . .

CAROL: Ooh, and you have toe hair! How virile. Lester always has to wear a little wig on his. Now, how about I draw you as Snidely Whiplash. He's the BAD character.

MAX: Uh, okay . . .

CAROL: (*She draws the face on his foot.*) We'll give him dark, piercing eyes and a wickedly handsome mustache . . .

MAX: (*Giggling.*) Ooh, ooh, that tickles!

CAROL: That's because you're new to it. Lester barely feels anything anymore. (*Beat.*) Now, let's give him an evil grin . . .

MAX: (*Despite himself.*) Hee-hee! I didn't realize my feet were so sensitive. Ooh! Wow . . . that's really an incredible sensation there . . . I can feel that all through my body. Wow . . .

CAROL: How about here?

MAX: Ooh! I . . . wow.

CAROL: You have really firm balls.

MAX: Uh, thanks. (*Beat.*) Nobody's ever touched them like that before.

CAROL: Now let's get started. Here's your Snidely Whiplash hat. (*She places it on his big toe, then settles back in her chair.*) Okay, put your foot up, and . . . action! (*Speaking in her Nell voice.*) Oh, you bad man! Let me go! Let me go!

MAX: (*Awkwardly moving his foot toward her and trying an evil voice.*) Ha, ha! I've got you now. You'll never get away.

CAROL: (*Pressing her foot up against his.*) You're not going to tie me up, are you?

MAX: (*Getting into it.*) Yes! I'm going to tie you up—tight! You're mine, you hear me? All mine!

CAROL: (*Caressing him with her toes.*) Oh, poor me! I'm helpless!

MAX: (*Caressing her back.*) Yes, yes you are!

> (*Their feet launch into a frenzied passion, rubbing over each other wildly and interlocking their toes.*)

MAX: (*Passionately.*)	CAROL:
. . . uh…OH! That's amazing . . . Ah, ah . . . wow . . . wow . . . yeah . . . It . . .	Ooh . . . yeah. Ooh . . . yeah! That's so good . . . Ooh, right there! Yes! Yes, that's it
OH . . . OH . . . OH . . . OHHHH!!!!	OH . . . OH . . . OH . . . OHHHH!!!!

CAROL: (*Orgasmically.*) My pinky toe! Oh god . . . MY—PINK—Y—TOE!!!

> (*The COORDINATOR comes running on followed by LESTER using a crutch.*)

COORDINATOR: (*Horrified.*) WHAT IS GOING ON HERE?!?

> (*She runs between them and separates their feet. Picking them up by their big toes, she stands facing out with each foot hanging limply from her fists.*)

What a disgrace! After all we've done to bring this art form out of the gutter! I should've known when I saw your pretty little feet. Now you leave me no choice. As Coordinator of the 14th Annual Puppet Festival, I hereby order you . . . de-faced.

CAROL: NO!

COORDINATOR: Yes. Lester, get the makeup remover.

> (*LESTER takes a makeup remover cloth and angrily wipes off CAROL's character face. CAROL watches in horror.*)

Carol, you are hereby banned from foot puppetry. (*She drops their feet.*) I want you both out of the theater. Lester, next year we will find you a new partner. One who better understands the purity of our art.

LESTER: Yes, Madame Coordinator. Thank you.

> (*He glares at CAROL a moment and then follows the COORDINATOR offstage. There is a long moment of silence as CAROL and MAX shamefully put on their socks and shoes. They avoid looking at each other.*)

MAX: (*After a moment.*) Uh . . . look, I'm sorry.

CAROL: No, it's my fault. I don't know what came over me.

MAX: You were just being . . . in the moment.

CAROL: (*Starting to cry.*) I don't what I'm going to do. Banned from foot puppetry! It's been my whole life.

MAX: Oh, hey . . . don't cry! (*He pats her shoulder.*) There are other forms of puppetry, you know. (*Beat.*) I'm actually pretty good at one.

CAROL: You? Really?

MAX: Yeah. But unfortunately, it's what landed me in jail. Indecent exposure. People are so limited in their thinking! What they don't realize is that you can make really wonderful puppets out of . . . (*He whispers in her ear.*)

CAROL: (*Shocked but excited.*) You can make puppets out of . . . THAT?

MAX: Yup. It's quite a delicate art form. Would you like me to teach you?

CAROL: Sure!

MAX: Great! Come on then, let's go . . . !

> (*He takes her hand and they run out smiling.*)

END OF PLAY

FROZEN FOODS

by Ian August

Frozen Foods was originally produced by Bill Wolski and Holly Baker-Kreiswirth for Little Fish Theatre's 2019 Pick of the Vine Short Play Festival, January 10 through February 3, 2019, at the Little Fish Theatre, 777 Centre Street, San Pedro, California.

The play was directed by Cinthia Palmer, featuring Holly Baker-Kreiswirth as CAROL, and Rachel Levy as LINDA. The production stage manager was Jacob Severence.

CHARACTERS

CAROL, 40s, mother and housewife.
LINDA, 40s, mother and housewife.

SETTING

Aisle 11 of the Superfood Market.

Time

Now-ish.

• • •

Lights up on the frozen foods aisle of the local Superfood Market, clear glass case doors line the path, each one containing brightly colored packages obscured by thin layers of frost. CAROL stands among them, a plastic basket at her feet. She holds a frozen TV dinner in her hands. She stares at it, blankly. She stares.

She stares.

CAROL: Four for the price of one.

(*LINDA, also a mother and housewife and part time real estate agent, enters. She sees CAROL.*)

LINDA: Carol? Is that you?

(*CAROL does not respond.*)

Oh my God, Carol? Carol! I haven't seen you since the PTA meeting three weeks ago! How have you been? How's Jessie? Has she had her ballet recital yet? I ended up returning the toe shoes and tutu when Virginia told me she would rather dig up moss in the cracks of the sidewalk than go back to ballet. I took her in the back yard and gave her a stick and watched her go to town. She was on the front stoop for nearly three hours. I practically read a whole novel! Well, it was a novella, but who's counting?

(*CAROL does not respond.*)

She is exhausting though—running around like she's being chased by a rabid ocelot. Zip! Zip! Zip! I literally fell asleep at Tiffany's birthday party at Funderland last week. Literally. Asleep. Standing. Next to the skee ball. Virginia and Molly from church found me passed out upright like a horse clutching a wad of tickets in my teeth and the straw from my Diet Sprite poking out of a hole in my sweater. Can you believe it? I looked insane!

(*CAROL does not respond.*)

Really insane! Hahaha!

(*She finally notices CAROL's catatonic gaze.*)

Carol? Carol, honey, are you okay?

(*CAROL does not respond.*)

Carol?

(*She reaches for the frozen dinner, and the moment she touches it, CAROL jolts upright. She looks up to LINDA.*)

CAROL: Linda?

LINDA: Carol? What . . . what happened?

CAROL: I . . . I don't know. I just . . . I just . . .

LINDA: Carol, are you okay? Do you want me to call the manager?

CAROL: No, I'm fine. Really, I am.

LINDA: You gave me quite a shock.

CAROL: I know.

LINDA: You looked all . . . stroke-y.

CAROL: I'm sorry.

LINDA: What was—what were you doing?

CAROL: Oh, Lin—Oh . . . I'm not sure. I remember I was standing here, looking for the Hungrifriend Dinners.

LINDA: I love those dinners.

CAROL: Me too.

LINDA: The Salisbury steak with the peas and carrots? Yum!

CAROL: I know.

LINDA: And look! They're on sale!

   (*CAROL blanches.*)

Four for the price of one!

CAROL: (*A realization.*) That's what it was!

LINDA: What what was?

CAROL: I was reaching in to grab a few Hungrifriend Dinners—the fried chicken ones that Bill likes best. The ones that have the little pocket of corn and the little pocket of potatoes and the tiny cocoa scented mock-brownie patty . . .

LINDA: Frank loves those, too.

CAROL: And then I remembered: I paid full price for those last week.

LINDA: I . . . I don't follow.

CAROL: Last week—last week I bought four of these Hungrifriend

Dinners—and they cost four dollars a box. I spent sixteen dollars on these last week. Sixteen! And today—I look over and see that they're four for four dollars? It's ridiculous!

LINDA: I know! What a deal!

CAROL: And then I thought, there must be something wrong with these. A lapsed expiration date, a reduced number of chicken bits, the potatoes are made of wallpaper paste. Why else would they be so much less expensive this week than last?

LINDA: It's just a sale, Carol. There are always sales on these things.

CAROL: But why? Why should they cost me a dollar a box this week when last week I spent four times as much? Who makes up those rules? Who gets to decide that the Hungrifriend Dinners I buy this week should be worth so much less than the ones from last week? And why are they so cheap? If there's nothing wrong with them—if they're the same boxed chicken dinners from last week—well then—what the hell is going on? It makes no sense! And then it came to me: (*She takes a pause. She looks up.*) There is no such thing as God.

(*Beat.*)

LINDA: What?

CAROL: Don't you see, Linda? If there was a God, if there was an almighty figure presiding over everything—every birth, every death—if there was a grand organizer up in heaven planning and plotting and dictating the motions of our existence—then how could that explain the randomness of it all? Four for the price of one? *Four* for the price of *one*?

LINDA: For God's sake, Carol—it's just a sale!

CAROL: But it isn't, is it? It's not just a sale. Because it's also children getting cancer and wars in the Middle East and famine and drought and flooding and tornadoes! It's the Thomases getting divorced and the giant goiter on Jenny Mueller's neck and that boy who lives down the street who has three eyes and seven nipples. It's random, don't you see, Linda? It's completely arbitrary! There's no plan, because there's no planner! God does not exist!

LINDA: I bet Pastor Jim wouldn't be too pleased to hear you say that.

CAROL: Fuck Pastor Jim, Linda! Fuck him right in the eye!

LINDA: Carol! People will hear you—

CAROL: And do you know why? Because if God doesn't exist, if God isn't real—and I'm pretty sure this . . . (*She grabs the frozen dinner from LINDA's hand and shakes it in the air.*) . . . proves that God isn't real—then what *is* real? What is reality?

LINDA: Carol—you—you're talking nonsense!

CAROL: Am I, Lin? Or are you even here? Are you real, Linda?

LINDA: Of course I'm real! I'm buying stool softeners! Why would I do that if I weren't real?

CAROL: Maybe, Linda, maybe you don't exist. Maybe none of this exists. This basket, this dinner, this entire aisle is a series of electrical currents in my brain attempting to convince me that it's all real. But none of it—not even you—exist.

(*The lights begin to shift.*)

You are simply a series of random signals to my brain. You only exist if I can perceive you. The minute I turn—

(*She does so—only the objects in front of her remain in light. Everything else is bathed in darkness.*)

The objects behind me cease to be. And when I turn the other way . . .

(*She does so—only the objects in front of her remain in light. Everything else is bathed in darkness.*)

The world appears to me born anew, and the things I no longer observe are gone forever.

LINDA: But they're not, Carol—they're all still there!

CAROL: Says the voice inside my brain that I have recently named "Linda."

LINDA: That was my grandmother's name!

CAROL: Your grandmother doesn't exist. The world in which I live is confined to my ability to perceive it. If I do not see it, it cannot be. I am at the center of the universe!

(*She turns out to the audience. The stage becomes the darkness of space—*

*and millions of stars appear around them. LINDA stares out in wonder.
When they speak, their voices echo.)*

If I do not hear you, you have not spoken. If I do not see you, you are not
there. Even touch is not a touch—it is merely a false sensory experience
activated by stimulating the nerve endings on my fingertips and arms.

LINDA: This is like that Keanu Reeves movie.

CAROL: The one with the bus?

LINDA: The one with the robots.

CAROL: *The Notebook*?

LINDA: *The Notebook* had robots?

CAROL: I don't remember. I was pretty drunk.

LINDA: I think that was Ryan Gosling.

CAROL: Ryan Gosling had robots?

LINDA: I thought we were talking about Keanu Reeves!

CAROL: It doesn't matter. Neither of them exists.

LINDA: But Carol—if nothing exists but you—then how do you know if *you*
exist?

*(CAROL stops, stunned—behind her, a super nova suddenly bursts into
being, a brilliant explosion of light envelops the stage. And then darkness.)*

CAROL: Oh my God—you're right. I don't exist. There is nothing anywhere.
There is nothing anywhere.

*(CAROL and LINDA begin to float in the darkness. LINDA's voice
echoes.)*

LINDA: Carol!

CAROL: I thought I heard a voice. But I don't exist. Maybe the voice is the
only part of me that's real.

LINDA: Carol!

CAROL: Do I respond to it? Can I respond? Or is it just a gust of galactic wind, screaming my name into the nothingness of the universe?

LINDA: Carol! Goddammit! Listen to me!

CAROL: How foolish I was to think I could contain the universe within me. I know only too late that I am the neither the universe nor its vessel. I am merely an echo of its emptiness.

> (*LINDA slaps CAROL across the face with the Hungrifriend Dinner. The lights return to normal. LINDA and CAROL stand in the frozen food aisle of the Superfood Market. Beat.*)

That hurt.

LINDA: Then you exist, don't you?

CAROL: I, uh . . .

LINDA: You want me to slap your face again.

CAROL: No.

LINDA: Do you want me to step on your foot? Or punch your breast?

CAROL: Not really.

LINDA: Why not?

CAROL: It hurts.

LINDA: If it hurts, it's real. (*Beat.*) Carol, maybe you should go home and lie down for a while.

CAROL: Yes. You know? I think . . . I think you may be right. I think that might make me feel a bit better.

LINDA: Of course it will, hon.

CAROL: I just had a moment.

LINDA: I know. Like in that Keanu Reeves movie.

CAROL: The one with the space aliens?

LINDA: Be safe getting home. And give Bill and Jessie my love, okay?

CAROL: Okay.

LINDA: See you next week at the PTA meeting.

(CAROL doesn't answer. She exits, still a little dazed. LINDA watches her go, and then looks down at her hands. She holds the box of Hungrifriend Dinner. She looks at it, and reaches for the freezer case.)

Four for the price of one. (*She giggles. And then stops. She brings her hand back. She stares at the box in her hands.*) Four for the price of one. (*She stares.*)

(Blackout.)

END OF PLAY

GLASSTOWN

by Don Nigro

Glasstown was first presented by Nylon Fusion Theatre Company at TADA! at 15 West 28th Street in New York City on October 25, 2019, with the following cast:

MINNIE: Holly O'Brien
MAC: Eric Percival

It was directed by Ivette Dumeng.

CHARACTERS

MINNIE
MAC

• • •

The workroom/living room of a house in Armitage, Ohio. in the 1970s, where MINNIE and her husband MAC, a young couple, live. MAC is an artist who is currently collecting old store mannequins and blow-up dolls. MAC is building what appears to be a sort of fairly large birdhouse. MINNIE is on the sofa reading Wuthering Heights.

MINNIE: (*Puts down her book, looks at MAC.*) So, do you want to have sex?

MAC: What?

MINNIE: Reading *Wuthering Heights* always makes me horny.

MAC: I'm working.

MINNIE: Okay. Fine. I won't bother you. (*Pause.*) Did you know Emily Bronte had a brother?

MAC: I don't care.

MINNIE: She had four sisters and a brother but two sisters died at boarding school and their mother was also dead and they lived out on the heath with their father, who was a curate with a terrible temper who used to shoot at spots he thought were crawling on the walls, and Emily and the two sisters who weren't dead and their brother were so bored out there on the heath that they got together and made up a complete alternate universe to live in.

MAC: No they didn't.

MINNIE: No, it's true, I swear. They invented an imaginary place called Glasstown and all the people and the geography and everything and then they just all lived there.

MAC: So they were insane?

MINNIE: Pretty much, yes. (*Pause.*) Are you sure you don't want to have sex?

MAC: In a minute, all right?

MINNIE: Thank God the romance hasn't gone out of our marriage. What the hell are you making, that you'd rather work on than have sex? Is that a bird house? You'd rather make a bird house than have sex with me? What are we, like a hundred and twelve? Anyway, we already have a bird house. Except I think there's a rat living in there because the birds go in but they don't come out. What is that? A dollhouse?

MAC: It's a perspective box.

MINNIE: Well, good. We can use that, because perspective is important and I lost mine at the dog races.

MAC: The Dutch made them. You look in the peep hole and see another universe.

MINNIE: No, what is it really? Because if we put up another bird house we're probably just going to draw another rat.

(*Pause. MAC keeps working.*)

MINNIE: So that's got a peephole?

MAC: Yep.

MINNIE: I've always wanted a peephole. It sounds really dirty. You know that one-eyed boy from Shit Creek used to have two eyes until one day he was looking though a peephole in a fence at these girls swimming naked, and their brother jammed a screw driver in the other side of the hole and his eye popped like a plastic bag full of petroleum jelly. Can I look?

MAC: It's not done.

MINNIE: So?

MAC: My father told me, never show a fool a work half done.

MINNIE: Your father was an asshole. And I'm not a fool. Except I married you. Does that count?

MAC: All right. Look right in there.

MINNIE: That little hole?

MAC: Yes.

MINNIE: There's not a rat in there with a screwdriver, is there?

MAC: I don't think so.

MINNIE: All right. But if there is, and I've got to wear an eye patch for the rest of my life, you're going to have to buy me a parrot.

MAC: Okay.

MINNIE: (*Cautiously looking in the peep hole.*) Holy crap. Holy crap. It's like a whole—it's like Alice going through the looking glass. The detail in there is incredible. Can we just move in there? I need one of those Drink Me bottles that Alice drank so she could get in the little door. I mean, really, Mac, this is amazing. It's like a whole complete other house in there. It's like another dimension.

MAC: I know.

MINNIE: What are you going to do with this?

MAC: I don't know. Try to squeeze through the peephole and live in there, I guess.

MINNIE: This is so cool. (*Pause.*) Mac, what are you doing here?

MAC: What do you mean?

MINNIE: I mean what are you doing here? You're a really gifted artist. You could actually be famous or something. What are you doing hiding in an old house in the middle of rustic Ohio nowhere?

MAC: Where should I be?

MINNIE: I don't know. New York. Paris. Someplace where there's more people than cows.

MAC: I don't speak French, and I've been to New York. Didn't like it much.

MINNIE: You got scared, so you retreated back to what felt safe. Me.

MAC: I shouldn't have come back and married you?

MINNIE: I'm glad you came back. But I just don't see any future for you here.

MAC: I'm happy here.

MINNIE: If you're happy, then why are you fucking my sister?

MAC: Why am I what?

MINNIE: Why are you fucking my sister?

MAC: Which one?

MINNIE: You know which one.

MAC: That's crazy.

MINNIE: Don't tell me I'm crazy. I'm not crazy. Well, maybe I'm a little bit crazy, but that doesn't mean I'm also stupid and blind.

MAC: Where on earth did you ever get the idea . . .

MINNIE: Stop it. Don't sit there and lie to me, okay? Fucking my sister is one thing, but sitting there and lying to my face about it is worse. (*Pause.*) It's all right. I don't really care that much. I've decided to be Ida Lupino.

MAC: What?

MINNIE: Ida Lupino. I'm not going to be upset about you fucking my sister. I'm going to be Ida Lupino instead. I'm going to be smart and cool and I'm not going to be in other people's movies. From now on I'm going to direct my own damned movie. (*Pause.*) Look, I know I'm not easy. My sister is easy. I'm not. I know that period in which I was terrified to get out of bed because I was afraid the centipedes were trying to kill me was a little stressful for you. I can understand that. I can understand you getting exhausted with me and just wanting a simpler sort of relationship. And my sister is about as simple as you can get. The point is, you're not happy, or you wouldn't be jumping in the sack with a moron. And the reason you're not happy is that you made a mistake. You got to feeling overwhelmed in New York and you panicked and came home and married your childhood sweetheart and started collecting old department store mannequins and blow up dolls and making boxes you can look in and totally get lost in another universe. But it doesn't work. You can be the greatest artist in the history of the world and it's not going to matter because if you stay here nobody is ever going to see it. Don't stay here for me, and ruin your career, and then betray me with my sister and tell me it's all my fault.

MAC: It's not your fault.

MINNIE: I know it's not my fault. Other things are my fault. I don't want to talk about that. The point is, being a real artist isn't just about making things. It's about sharing them. You know what happened to Emily Bronte's brother, who stayed home and lived inside his own imaginary world? He drank himself to death. Emily and Charlotte and Anne all put themselves out there and took a chance, but he didn't. You don't want to be like him.

MAC: Minnie . . .

MINNIE: Ida. Call me Ida. I'm not Minnie anymore, okay? I'm directing my own movie now.

MAC: Ida, I'm staying right here, with you.

MINNIE: Because you're afraid.

MAC: Because I love you.

MINNIE: That is not a good reason. Especially when you're inserting your penis in my simple-minded sister.

MAC: I don't love your sister.

MINNIE: Well, I do, and you're not doing her any favors, either. An artist has got to have the courage to embrace their own madness. Anne wrote good novels. She had a modest gift, and she did what she could with it, which was quite a lot, actually. Charlotte was like half genius and half respectable Victorian crash dummy, so she wrote a novel which is great when she's trusting her madness but every now and then turns into conventional Victorian slop when she tries to have it both ways. But Emily, she trusted her madness. *Jane Eyre* is like seventy or eighty percent genius but twenty or thirty percent Victorian crap, but *Wuthering Heights* is all genius, every incredibly weird and convoluted square inch of it, because Emily didn't give a shit what anybody thought. She trusted her madness.

MAC: But didn't she stay home, too?

MINNIE: Yes. And it killed her.

MAC: Or trusting her madness killed her. (*Pause.*) I don't care. I'm not going anywhere.

MINNIE: Well, you can do what you want. I'm trusting my own madness. I'm going through the looking glass and being Ida Lupino.

MAC: Minnie . . .

MINNIE: I can't hear you. I've gone back into my own personal perspective box. You can come if you want. We'll both live in Glasstown, where you can pretend to be a genius living in a converted barn in Ohio and I can pretend you're not fucking my sister. Glasstown is actually a really nice place. Except that it's entirely constructed of lies.

(*They look at each other. The light fades on them and goes out.*)

END OF PLAY

THE GRAVE, THE FAN, THE WIFE

by Dorian Palumbo

Presented by Darknight Productions as part of their one-act series "Four Women Only" on Friday, April 5, and Saturday, April 6, 2019, at the Playroom Theater, 151 West 46th Street, 8th Floor, New York, New York.

The play starred Ruth Kavanagh as PETRA NOBLE, and Meredith Rust as SAMARA FINNERTY. Ruth Kavanagh appeared via waiver from Actor's Equity.

Directed by Dorian Palumbo

CHARACTERS

SAMARA FINNERTY, 50s. In her prime, she was probably a Ramones girl, complete with dog collar and a mohawk. Now, in middle age, she's toned it down, but certainly not all the way.
PETRA NOBLE, 50s, English, well dressed and self-possessed. You could not imagine her ever losing an argument.

SETTING

The untended grave of Billy Noble, film and television actor. The plot should be covered with dead grass into which SAMARA can haphazardly plant lavender stalks.

NOTE

The author would like to encourage diverse casting.

• • •

A graveyard, the English countryside, dusk. Lights up on: SAMARA FINNERTY, 50s, American, is kneeling and tending a grave which has apparently been utterly neglected. She is tattooed and her hair is dyed several shades of unnatural; we can imagine that she was a punk in the 80s. The simple headstone says only "Billy Noble" and, below his name, "Actor." SAMARA is trying to plant lavender on the very resistant grave—she's only got her two hands and what looks like a ballpoint pen to dig with, and the stalks seem determined to fall over; she waters them anyway, with water from a plastic bottle. Near the headstone, there is another bottle—whisky, judging by the color. The lavender falls over again.

SAMARA: Stay up, goddamn it.

> *(Enter PETRA, 50s, tastefully dressed—as if she could be a member of Parliament during the week and is now wearing her country weekend ensemble. SAMARA is too busy trying to dig a deeper hole for the lavender to notice PETRA standing over her at first. Finally, she looks up.)*

I know, I'm probably not doing this right.

PETRA: You seem to be doing all right to me. Nice space between the plants. You could do with a spade or something.

SAMARA: I asked the gravedigger guy in the booth down the hill if he had something like that. I figured he would, but he says he doesn't, he just has this massive shovel and it just, I don't know, it seemed kinda disrespectful.

PETRA: Indeed it would be.

SAMARA: That's what I thought. *(She continues working.)* English lavender. Well, you know, he was English.

PETRA: We're in England, so I suppose that's quite a good guess.

SAMARA: Oh, I don't have to guess. We were friends.

PETRA: Oh, were you?

SAMARA: Yes, very close friends.

PETRA: Close friends as in, well, you know . . . (*She tosses her head in what she probably thinks is a seductive way. SAMARA gets the message.*)

SAMARA: Oh, no, no, we never did that, no. Billy had problems. Well, he was married, well, he was with someone for a really long time, and then they got married at the end there. I guess it made sense at that point.

PETRA: Perhaps so, yes.

SAMARA: You know, the gravedigger guy, he said Billy's wife hasn't bothered to take care of this little grave at all, it's like the bitch doesn't even care.

PETRA: Well, perhaps she's not sentimental about the dead body of a raging alcoholic.

(*SAMARA looks up at PETRA, as if seeing her for the first time. She clambers to her feet to face PETRA.*)

SAMARA: Oh, shit, man, I am so sorry. You're her. You're Pee-tra.

PETRA: Petra.

SAMARA: Ah, jeez, I'm sorry. Petra.

PETRA: And, no, all this is fine, really. Billy hated lavender, he hated any flower with scent, so chucking lavender all over his grave is something I would have done myself if I'd thought of it.

SAMARA: Did he hate it? Seriously? I should probably just pull it up.

PETRA: Darling, please, it was a lovely gesture. More than he deserved. If any other of his fans come by, I suppose they'll enjoy them. (*She kneels down part way and runs her fingers over one of the lavender plants.*)

SAMARA: He brought joy into people's lives all over the world. The roles he played. Podge Hanrahan, and Prince Michael in the Dover Diary?

PETRA: Oh, good Lord.

SAMARA: Good Lord is right. And when Captain Carter told Gemma Manford that he'd rather never see her again if that was what she needed to make her happy, oh, jeez Louise, that just about ripped your guts out watching that.

PETRA: You know that was acting, don't you? I mean, he was an actor. You pretend that you feel things.

SAMARA: Oh, well, acting isn't that easy, you know? You can't just fake all of it. Some of it has to be real. Nobody's that good.

PETRA: I wouldn't expect you to understand, you were one of his fans. There's a version of Billy inside your head that you invest with all sorts of virtues and qualities that, I can assure you, he never had.

SAMARA: He had lots of good qualities, I know he did. He was smart, he was well read. He was funny and warm. He had that, what is that word, the vulna-bility, those big eyes, man, you just look at those eyes and you know there was a sad story he didn't dare tell you. (*She stands and turns her back on PETRA for a moment.*)

PETRA: Billy confessed to me once, after he'd been on location, that the production company had sent a driver to take him to the hotel, and "she was so young and winsome," he "couldn't help seducing her" and he was oh so sorry he'd fucked her in the middle of the Irish bogland someplace. Well, after I was through being gob-smacked, I said, "Billy, you prat, they sent you a prostitute so you wouldn't be manic on the set next morning." Do you know what he said to me? He said, "Oh, Petra, hookers don't drive." He was a bloody lunatic. And you all thought he was exactly like the romantic heroes he pretended to be in one cheap film after another. Fan. Short for "fanatic."

SAMARA: Hey, listen, go ahead and feel superior making me look stupid, that ain't so hard. I'm forty-nine years old and I can barely get a passport and get myself on a plane to come over here. I got a shitty job at a rundown old hospital, and, shit, I can't even make a fucking plant stand up straight.

(*She touches the poor little droopy plant. PETRA kneels down next to her.*)

PETRA: Every once in a while I like to check Billy's old Facebook page and see what his admirers are saying about him. Today I ran across someone chastising me for not visiting this grave. And they also said my photograph made me look "chunky" which I did not appreciate. (*Beat.*)

SAMARA: You were wearing horizontal stripes.

PETRA: That's your response to me? Right here, to my face?

SAMARA: I'm sorry.

PETRA: That shift was vintage Yves Saint Laurent.

SAMARA: Yeah, whatever.

PETRA: Oh, what do you know about fashion. You're American. You show up for job interviews in a t-shirt and a leotard.

SAMARA: Yeah, see all this? (*Indicates her clothes.*) This is Je Ce la Pennet, bitch. And you know what? Ain't got no horizontal stripes, 'cause every girl over the age of ten knows that shit makes you look fat.

PETRA: You don't know what an absolute shit Bill could be. Well, of course you don't, you don't want to know. I suppose it was nice to think about someone like Billy, even if Billy wasn't really like that.

SAMARA: Don't you patriotize me.

PETRA: Patronize.

SAMARA: Don't correct me, neither.

PETRA: Sorry.

SAMARA: S'okay.

PETRA: He had a horrible temper, you know. The neighbors in Fulham used to complain about the shouting, the neighbors in New York used to complain about the shouting and everyone shouts in New York. The only place they didn't seem to mind was the condominium in Tuscany, and that's probably because Italians actually enjoy shouting. That's why they invented the opera, for God's sake.

SAMARA: It was probably the alcohol. Mood swings, right?

PETRA: Ah. So you did know.

> (*SAMARA picks up a sprig of lavender and sniffs it, pretending to ignore PETRA for a moment.*)

Billy would start with the wine when we were out, then he'd end the night with just a little whiskey, darling, just a drop, just a wee dram darling. And then we'd scuttle home in a cab, not talking. I knew he was longing to get home and start a bender. I was in the process of divorcing him when he passed away. Oh, yes. I told myself I wasn't really divorcing Bill. I was divorcing the alcoholic that was holding Bill hostage. But Bill and the alcoholic were one and the same. It wasn't a part he was playing. Perhaps if I'd been a bit stronger, somehow, he would have done something about it eventually and we'd have survived, but I just couldn't take it.

SAMARA: No one can take that. You'd have to be a canonized saint to take that kind of shit.

PETRA: He used to call me a saint sometimes. "My wife is a saint." I was nothing of the kind. Poor auld Bill.

(SAMARA stands and begins to open the bottle, then stops.)

SAMARA: I guess I should pour this out, but I'm ashamed to say it cost me twenty pounds and I just don't feel like it.

(PETRA holds out her hand for the bottle, which SAMARA gives over reluctantly. PETRA opens the bottle and takes a healthy draught. SAMARA sits back down beside PETRA and takes a drink.)

SAMARA: We wasn't really friends, Billy and me.

PETRA: I know.

SAMARA: I did meet him, once, though. I did. I went to see him down at this Comic Con in Tallahassee, that's where I'm from, I'm from Florida. Woodville, 'bout ten miles from Tallahassee. I'd never been to one of those things, I asked my friend Eva to come along, she didn't know who the heck Billy was, she'd just do anything to get out of the house. Anyway, I didn't really want to just wade in with all the rest of the kooks and make Billy sign some dumb ole picture or whatnot. Me and Eva, we just kinda stood back and watched him while he sat at the table and smiled and laughed and signed for this one or that. Being so sweet and everything. That was the real Billy Noble to me, the guy who asked each fan a question while he was signing the DVD for 'em, looked 'em right in the eye waiting for the answer. Then he was done signing autographs, Billy's line was shorter than some of the other stars, I felt bad about that I remember, Billy went off behind this curtain thing and disappeared off somewhere, me and Eva went over to the Hotel Duval to get us a cocktail, and right there at the bar, there was Billy. He was sitting at the end of the bar, you know, all by himself. The bar's on a rooftop. Wasn't even looking at the view, he was just sipping his whisky and staring at the wall. Eva didn't even catch on at first, you know, she's all self-absorbed and stuff, but she must have seen me looking at him and then she says, like, "Hey, that's him, that's the guy." And I go, "Yeah, uh-huh, that's him all right." That's him. That's Billy Noble. Eva's all pushing me to go talk to him, and I'm like, nah, I don't want to bother him, but, you know, finally I did bunch up the old courage, swallow it down, and I go over there thinking, well, I'll just say hello, and that I'm a big fan, and thank him for coming all the way to Tallahassee to see us.

PETRA: And did you say that?

SAMARA: I did. You know what he said to me?

PETRA: What?

SAMARA: He said "fuck off." I guess I didn't move for a second, I was just kinda stunned or something. He looks up at me, and he says it again, he says, "Go on. Fuck off." And then just goes back to sippin' his whiskey.

PETRA: Yes, well, that sounds like Bill all right.

SAMARA: When I got back to the table, Eva asked me how it was, and I just had to make somethin' up, you know, I wasn't gonna tell her what really happened, she mighta tried to get up in his face or something. Eva's that friend, you know that one girlfriend you have if somebody buys her a shot of tequila, eventually y'all are just going to jail?

PETRA: Ah, yes.

SAMARA: Anyway, Eva, she asked me how it went, I said he was fine, that he was getting a cold or something, so he couldn't talk too long. I said he asked me where I was from, 'bout his movies. I lied, I made it all up, and she gives me a hug starts jumping around and I just felt like a piece of dirt but I had to smile and laugh. And then, 'course it's Eva, she just goes back to talkin' about herself, so I was off the hook 'til she dropped me off home.

PETRA: Oh, dear.

SAMARA: When you're fans of some actor like Billy Noble, and you never met 'im, you do wonder what it would be like if they said something directly to you in conversation. "What exactly would he say to me?" You never think in a hundred years it's gonna be "fuck off," but I knew it was the whiskey talkin', so, after a while, I found it in my heart to forgive. Like I said, he couldn't-a played all those parts if there wasn't some piece of him in there that was still sweet. Kindly. Somewhere back of the booze, he had to still be in there.

(*PETRA gets to her feet, then holds out a hand to SAMARA.*)

PETRA: Come on. Come with me.

SAMARA: Where're we going?

PETRA: I'm going to take you to this marvelously snotty place called The Ivy. We're going to see lots of celebrities eating lunch, although you probably won't recognize most of them because they'll be British celebrities and not American ones.

SAMARA: I'm not dressed for that kind of thing, though.

PETRA: 'Course you are. We'll just tell everyone you're a writer. They never know how to dress themselves.

SAMARA: Can you just be nice without being mean underneath it?

PETRA: I really am the only English person you know. (*She grabs SAMARA by the sleeve.*) Come on, then.

(*SAMARA comes along for a moment, then hops back to put what's left of the whiskey back nestled in front of Billy's headstone.*)

(*Lights down.*)

END OF PLAY

THE HANSON KID

by Avery Bufkin

Produced by Moonlight Theater Company
Athens, Georgia
August 29 and 30, 2019

Directed by Elizabeth Kelley

ISAAC: Jim Morrison
DICKY: Nicholas Hemerling
CONNOR: Thompson Sewell

CHARACTERS

ISAAC, 60s.
DICKY, 30s.
CONNOR, 17.

SETTING

ISAAC's living room, with a counter full of photographs and various knick-knacks, a lamp.

TIME

Now.

NOTE

A slash / indicates an overlap.

• • •

ISAAC and DICKY sit opposite one another as they stare around in silence. The lights are dim. It's dark outside.

DICKY: It's getting dark.

ISAAC: The sun's gone down.

DICKY: Can't see for shit. (*He gets up and flips on the lamp.*)

ISAAC: It might take a while. Sometimes he doesn't come until after midnight.

DICKY: Don't worry. We'll get him. We'll get this bastard.

ISAAC: "Get him." I don't want to "get him." What does that mean? I just / want to help . . .

(*DICKY pulls a gun out from inside his jacket, holds it up, then returns it to his pocket. Beat.*)

What the hell.

DICKY: This is justice.

ISAAC: You're not shooting / this kid.

DICKY: I'm not shooting anyone. It's not loaded. They're blanks. It's part of the game. This'll scare the shit out of this guy.

ISAAC: Right. Fine.

DICKY: Does he smash the windows? Pee on the carpets?

ISAAC: Does he what?

DICKY: I'm trying to get a sense of this guy. I need to get in his head.

ISAAC: Oh. He likes to mess with photos over there.

DICKY: These photos?

ISAAC: Yeah, those photos. He likes to move them around.

(DICKY walks over to the back counter and starts moving the photographs around.)

Sometimes he eats the food.

DICKY: So, he eats your food, moves your pictures. Take anything? What's he stealing?

ISAAC: Oh, just petty cash, usually. Once he took a watch, but he brought it back the next day. My wife / used to . . .

DICKY: Give me a second. I need some quiet. I need a lot of quiet.

ISAAC: I like to sit in the quiet, too.

DICKY: Really.

ISAAC: It's most of what I do in a day. (*Beat.*) How much do I owe you for this?

DICKY: You know, normally I'd say five hundred. I'd look at you, and I'd think: This guy doesn't know the value of money.

ISAAC: Right.

DICKY: This guy can't hear. He doesn't know.

ISAAC: I can hear.

DICKY: I'd think: This guy's easy pickings. But I'm not going to say that to you because now I want to get this son-of-a-bitch. You've recruited me.

ISAAC: Right.

DICKY: So we'll say four-fifty.

ISAAC: Wow. That's more than I expected.

DICKY: Do you want to catch this bastard? Let's get tough on crime, how 'bout it? How 'bout we actually punish trespassers and thieves?

ISAAC: I just want to / scare him.

DICKY: Look. Look. This guy's been coming around for too long. Messing with your things. Eating your food. Walking around in your home, alright? While you're in bed sleeping, alright? Am I scaring you? It's scaring the shit out of me.

ISAAC: Well, he's just a / kid, so . . .

DICKY: Let's get some things straight: First, I usually get paid up front.

ISAAC: Oh, right, yeah . . .

(*Something breaks offstage.*)

What was that? Did you hear that?

DICKY: I hear everything.

ISAAC: Right. 'Cause sometimes my hearing's a bit . . .

DICKY: Yeah, yeah, yeah. That's why I'm here. You need ears. And eyes. And legs. You need everything. I've got this.

ISAAC: I can walk.

DICKY: I've got this. I've got your legs. I'm your legs now. And your ears. And your eyes. I'm you now.

ISAAC: Right.

(*A sound is heard again offstage.*)

DICKY: I'm gonna check this.

ISAAC: I'll keep a lookout here, I guess.

DICKY: Good for you. That's good for you. You be you here, and I'll go be you out there.

ISAAC: Right, okay. But you can just be you out there, right?

DICKY: ???

ISAAC: Just thinking we can be ourselves. Probably best just to be ourselves. You don't really want to be me, I don't think.

DICKY: No. I didn't really want to be you, to be frank. Sorry to break it to you. You can take your legs. And your eyes. And your ears.

ISAAC: Thank you.

(*Sound heard offstage.*)

DICKY: You heard that?

ISAAC: I did.

(DICKY exits. ISAAC gets up and begins to put the photographs back in order. CONNOR enters. He freezes upon seeing Isaac.)

You better watch it. I'll call for Dicky.

CONNOR: Who's that?

(As if in answer to his question: gunshots and DICKY's are voice heard offstage.)

DICKY: *(Off.)* I've got him. That son-of-a-bitch. I've got him. *(Beat.)* Not him. Not this time. But I'm onto him. I'm onto him.

(Isaac finishes arranging his things and sits back down.)

ISAAC: You really better watch it 'cause Dicky won't be watching it. I'm the only one watching, and I'm not about to get up again for no one.

DICKY: *(Off.)* A mutt. Goddamn it. He had rabies. Isaac! He had rabies!

CONNOR: Close your eyes.

(ISAAC closes his eyes. CONNOR approaches the counter and begins to rearrange the photos.)

ISAAC: Now nobody's watching. Do you think Dicky's gonna come back in here, eyes all open and watching?

CONNOR: You're never up this late. *(Beat.)* So, why are you up this late?

ISAAC: You're supposed to be scared. I was trying to scare you straight.

CONNOR: I am scared.

ISAAC: No, you're not scared. *(Pause.)* He was in the war with my son. Dicky was in the war with my son.

CONNOR: Which war?

(He stares at one of the photographs. He picks it up.)

ISAAC: I asked him to come over to scare you straight. But I think he's gone mad.

(Gunshots offstage.)

CONNOR: I think he just shot another dog.

ISAAC: They're just blanks. (*Beat.*) I put some cash in the top drawer for you.

> (*CONNOR goes to it, checks the drawer, and grabs the money. He starts moving ISAAC's things around.*)

If you'd leave everything else where it is.

> (*CONNOR picks up an egg-shaped object.*)

CONNOR: What is this thing? I always wanted to ask, but you're usually asleep when I come by, and now I'm thinking: There you are.

ISAAC: Here I am.

CONNOR: And I'm thinking: Is this a fancy egg? What the hell is this guy doing with a fancy egg?

ISAAC: It's a box. If you twist it, the top'll pop off.

> (*CONNOR twists the top off with a "pop" sound.*)

Yeah, just like that. It pops off, and there's toothpicks inside.

CONNOR: Weird. (*He stares at the photographs.*) Haven't seen this one before. Ugly baby.

ISAAC: Which one? Our family's known for it.

CONNOR: Got him dressed in this polka-dot hat with these matching polka-dot pajamas.

ISAAC: Oh, my grandniece. That's the word, right? She's my nephew's baby. I think the word is grandniece.

CONNOR: Yeah, that's the word.

> (*DICKY enters, gun raised.*)

Holy shit.

> (*DICKY fires, clipping CONNOR's shoulder.*)

ISAAC: What happened to "unloaded," huh? What happened to "it's just blanks in this goddamn son-of-a-bitch?"

DICKY: Who is that? Is that a fucking kid?

ISAAC: You shot the Hanson's kid.

DICKY: Breaking and entering. Breaking and entering. That little bastard. What a kid. I always say: Never go in alone. You never know who's hiding behind that door with a loaded gun.

ISAAC: "Loaded gun." You son-of-a-bitch. You want to call for an ambulance? Drop the gun, Dicky!

DICKY: Hey, kid: Look at me. You're seeing me. Right? Yes. This is how you scare a kid straight, Isaac. You look him in the eye. You tell him what's up. Go on. Tell him. What's your name? The Hanson kid. Not a smart move, Hanson kid.

(DICKY exits as lights dim on ISAAC kneeling on the floor beside CONNOR, who sits up against the counter.)

END OF PLAY

HEAD SPACE

by Cynthia Faith Arsenault

Originally produced June 7, 8, 14, and 15, 2019, by Cannon Theatre, Littleton, Massachusetts.

Cast:
EVE: Debbie Crane
ADAM: Jim Hunt
ALTER EVE: Anne Dowell
ALTER ADAM: Bob Amici

Director: Maren Caufield
Producers: Chris Merritt and Tara Earl

CHARACTERS

EVE, 20–50, dressed for a date, on her best behavior, a bit of an effort, but
    wants this to go well.
ADAM, 20–50, jeans, more casual than EVE, here at his mother's behest,
    initially just wants it to be over.
ALTER EVE, 20–50, in a black body stocking or dressed same as EVE.
ALTER ADAM, 20–50, in a black body stocking or dressed same as ADAM.

SETTING

A high top table in the lounge/bar of a restaurant.

TIME

The present.

NOTE

At no time do either ADAM or EVE see or register the presence of each other's ALTERs. Unless otherwise noted, ADAM and EVE speak exclusively to each other.

ADAM and EVE can hear only their own ALTERs, who speak exclusively as a subconscious voice to them—this must be very clear. This is true throughout, until the very end, when the ALTERs finally see and address each other.

• • •

EVE is nervously seated, nursing a martini. ADAM rushes in, composes himself before she sees him; strolls over to the table and peers around from behind before approaching her, then tentatively asks:

ADAM: Eve?

EVE: Yes? Oh, yes! That's me. Right. Eve.

ADAM: Sorry I'm late.

(*EVE glances at her watch or phone to see the time, feigning surprise.*)

EVE: You're late?

(*ALTER EVE charges in next to EVE, skeptically looks ADAM up and down and baldly asserts.*)

ALTER EVE: Fifteen frigging minutes late!! Seriously? You don't own a phone?

ADAM: Sorry, traffic was horrendous.

(*ALTER ADAM strolls in and stands behind or to the side of ADAM and loudly whispers to him.*)

ALTER ADAM: Should I tell her why I'm really late? Honesty good. (*An indecisive beat.*) No, don't.

EVE: So you drove here?

ALTER EVE: Points for a guy with wheels, but prod for more info—
Mustang? BMW? Mercedes?

ADAM: Uh . . . Uber.

ALTER ADAM: Ugh, why'd I say that?

EVE: Hmm, I hoped you had a car.

ADAM: Oh, I did . . . I do.

ALTER ADAM: Quick—think, cover it!

ADAM: Uh . . . I mean . . . battery issues.

ALTER ADAM: "Battery issues"? No way she bought that—not to mention,
even if true, it'd be the least of my issues.

ADAM: Maybe I should sit down.

EVE: Oh, sure . . . yeah, sit—I, uh, just ordered a drink, because . . . well,
after ten minutes, I couldn't stand the server's hairy eyeball.

> (ADAM sits at the table.)

ADAM: Server? Where? I could sure use another—I mean, a drink! One
drink, my first today!

ALTER ADAM: Shit, Adam, back peddling much? Negative points on that
blurt. Good thing I remembered my Altoids. Oh, no, did I?!

> (He pats down ADAM's pockets, looking for mints, as EVE looks around
> for the server.)

EVE: Isn't that always the way? Servers are totally MIA when you want to
order, but then right there, interrupting, when you don't want that, like at
the punch line of a joke . . .

ALTER EVE: (Looking at her nails.) Yawn! Was that supposed to be witty?

ADAM: Exactly! And by the time you get back to it, no one remembers the
set up.

EVE: Right—it's all in the timing.

ALTER ADAM: Hmmm, kinda easy to talk to her. This isn't too bad . . . but
don't get my hopes up. Fix-ups are always disasters.

ALTER EVE: Hmm . . . he isn't too bad . . . but fix-ups, especially from mother, are always disasters. (*Pause.*)

EVE: Yeah, so . . . I guess our mothers know each other from Mahjong.

ALTER EVE: Why'd I say that?

ADAM: Ma who?

ALTER ADAM: Why'd I say that?! Was that supposed to be funny? (*Looking around.*)

Where's that server when you need interrupting?

ADAM: That was lame. Sorry.

ALTER ADAM: Stop with the "Sorry" already! How many times have we covered this? "Do NOT self-deprecate. Just keep moving."

ADAM: But perhaps a sign of good character to be able to laugh at yourself.

ALTER ADAM: Or brag. Do you ever listen to me?

ADAM: (*Turns slightly and to ALTER ADAM.*) Bug out!

EVE: Excuse me?!

ADAM: Bug!! I thought I saw a bug. Out. There! Warning! Bug out over there! Boy, you wouldn't expect an infestation in place like this . . . maybe we should go somewhere else.

ALTER EVE: Yeah, maybe we should go home and call it a night! Get in our PJs, tear open the Cheetos and red wine, and watch an old movie.

EVE: (*Scowling at ALTER EVE; turning back to ADAM.*) No, let's give it a chance.

ALTER EVE: We always settle! And waste too much time on losers. Remember tonight's pre-game discussion. Beat feet, if it's tanking.

EVE: (*Whispering loudly to ALTER EVE.*) I didn't say it was tanking.

ADAM: I know. I thought you said, "Let's give it a chance."

ALTER ADAM: Chance? Tank? They don't even rhyme. What's going on here? She's toying with us.

EVE: That is exactly what I said: "Give it a chance."

ALTER EVE: But not what we're thinking! Why are you going all rogue on me?

EVE: I know what I'm thinking!!

ADAM: I would hope so. I mean, I take you at your word.

ALTER ADAM: But what's her word? Maybe we should bail with our dignity relatively intact. Ready? Think of a good excuse! (*Pause.*)

EVE: So . . . uh, my mother said you live on the West Side.

ALTER EVE: Now you're on it! No more wasting time. Get the facts. Screen for independent living.

EVE: Condo or apartment?

ALTER EVE: Clever.

ADAM: Oh . . . uh-huh.

ALTER ADAM: Danger—move off topic—fast!

EVE: Uh-huh?! Which?

ALTER EVE: You go girl, hold his feet to that fire! Still not buying that battery excuse.

EVE: Condo or apartment?

ADAM: Uh . . . both, uh . . . neither. (*Pause.*) Uh, I have my own apartment in mom's condo basement.

ALTER ADAM: Argh!!!!! Way too much info—what the hell?

EVE: Well . . . truthful.

ALTER EVE: We cornered him! What else could he do?

ADAM: Lost points on that one?

ALTER ADAM: Again with the blurting! How many times have we covered this? Damn it, Adam!

EVE: No, truthful is good.

ADAM: (*To ALTER ADAM.*) See!!

ALTER EVE: A luxury apartment downtown is better. Let's ditch this loser and get back on Match.

ADAM: How about you?

ALTER ADAM: Good move—Turn those tables! And women always prefer to talk about themselves! So a two-fer!

ADAM: You live downtown?

EVE: Me? No. I live with my mom, too. I can't afford my own place, and I lived with way too many messy roommates—clothes strewn everywhere, hair in the shower drain, obnoxious boyfriends. It's so hard to get along with people sometimes . . . looking for that one person I sync with, before I move out again.

> *(ALTER EVE reaches from behind EVE and puts her hand over her mouth.)*

ALTER EVE: Are you insane?! TMI!! (*Pause.*) I'm not helping here—taking a bathroom break. (*Exiting, while talking over her shoulder to EVE, shaking her head.*) I'll catch up with you later.

EVE: What's the point of blind dating, if we don't put our cards on the table right away?

ADAM: You know, my thought exactly. It only makes sense.

ALTER ADAM: Sincere. Compassionate. Agreeable.

ADAM: Right!

EVE: Agreeing with yourself?

ADAM: If I don't believe in me, who can I trust?

EVE: What I say all the time.

ADAM: To who?

EVE: To who what?

ADAM: What you say—who to?

EVE: Oh . . . oh, to me . . . I have the best conversations with myself.

ADAM: Uh . . .

ALTER ADAM: Multiple personality alert!! Run! Run!

ALTER EVE: (*Rushing in, as she hears the last comment.*) Geesh, I leave for one minute, and he's ready to call the mental health hotline.

ADAM: Do you actually hear yourself talking?

EVE: (*Laughing.*) Only in my head.

ADAM: Oh . . . yeah—that! I know what you mean.

EVE: You do?

ADAM: I'm my own best audience. (*Laughs.*) But this isn't too bad either.

EVE: Yeah, this is different. I'm actually having a good time.

ADAM: Me too! (*Looking for the server.*) All the same, a drink wouldn't be bad.

EVE: Here, have some of mine. (*She proffers her drink to ADAM. He takes a sip and smiles.*)

ADAM: You drink Absolut Pepper, too?

EVE: Is there anything better?!

ADAM: Only thing would be food to go with it!

EVE: Oh, yes! Where is that server?

ADAM: I'm starved.

ALTER EVE: OK. You go girl, that was code for—he's starved for you.

EVE: (*Grabbing the menu.*) Everything looks delicious tonight.

ALTER ADAM: Everything! OK! That was code for you. The eagle has landed. You can take it from here.

ALTER EVE: That's the idea. I've been running the show behind the scenes, the whole—well, most of the time. Where'd you come from?

ALTER ADAM: Same gig! But now . . . my work's done here. Punching out.

ALTER EVE: Me too. (*She turns to leave, but turns back to ALTER ADAM.*)

ALTER EVE: How about a drink to wrap up a challenging day?

ALTER ADAM: I'm in.

ALTER EVE: I'm in.

> *(The ALTERs stroll off the stage, enamored of each other. ADAM signals the server, then nods as he anticipates the approach.)*

EVE: Great timing—we're just getting to the punch line.

END OF PLAY

HOT LOVE IN THE MOONLIGHT

by Patrick Gabridge

Hot Love in the Moonlight was commissioned by the Friends of Mount Auburn Cemetery as part of their artists-in-residence program. The play was first produced by Plays in Place at the Boston Theater Marathon at the Wimberly Theatre at the Stanford Calderwood Pavilion/Boston Center for the Arts on May 19, 2019, and then ran in a site-specific production at Mount Auburn Cemetery in Cambridge, Massachusetts, opening May 30, 2019, with the following team:

Cast:
MAC: Ed Hoopman
JEREMY: Jacob Oommen Athyal
SAMANTHA: Theresa Hoa Nguyen

Director: Courtney O'Connor
Costume Designer: Kimberly Berry
Sound Designer: Arshan Gailus
Stage Manager: Adele Nadine Traub
Assistant Stage Manager: Betsy Pierce
Associate Producer: Lindsay Eagle
Publicity: Rachel Lucas

CHARACTERS

MAC, a male spotted salamander. Not his first mating season. Might be a bit older than the other two.

JEREMY, a male spotted salamander. Nervous and inexperienced but wants to make a good impression. Definitely his first mating season. Close to the same age as Samantha, perhaps just a tiny bit younger.

SAMANTHA, a female spotted salamander. She's been through this before. Not sure about this year. Not sure about a lot of things.

SETTING

The shore of Consecration Dell at Mount Auburn Cemetery, a vernal pool in a historic cemetery.

TIME

A moonlit spring night.

NOTE

Though the characters are salamanders, there is no need to give them "realistic" salamander costumes, tails, etc. In fact, you're much better off avoiding such things altogether.

• • •

The vernal pool in Consecration Dell, at Mt. Auburn Cemetery. It is a warmish and wet spring night. JEREMY, a male spotted salamander, stands anxiously near the edge of the pool. Another male salamander, MAC, slowly walks down the path.

MAC: Yo! What up, dude?

JEREMY: Hey.

MAC: What a night, huh?

JEREMY: Yeah.

MAC: Perfect for a little mating action. This salamander is ready for some "liebespiel." Ya know?

JEREMY: Right. That is so right.

MAC: Don't look so nervous. The ladies want a man who shows some confidence.

JEREMY: Sure. Yeah. Confidence.

MAC: First mating season?

JEREMY: Could be.

MAC: Don't sweat it, dude. When it all gets rolling, just put out your best moves. This is your chance to perpetuate the species. You're gonna do fine. Speaking of fine, you seen any honeys yet?

JEREMY: Honeys?

MAC: Female spotted salamanders! Our very reason for existence!

JEREMY: Not yet.

MAC: They always take their time. I'm going in. Maybe some of the other guys are here already. Don't sweat it. If you don't get picked this year, at least you tried.

> (*He exits, into the pool. JEREMY waits, even more nervous than before. SAMANTHA, a female spotted salamander, emerges into the moonlight. Slowly. Takes a look around. JEREMY approaches SAMANTHA.*)

JEREMY: Hey, Baby.

SAMANTHA: Hi.

JEREMY: Quite a night.

SAMANTHA: Yeah.

JEREMY: Warm. And wet.

SAMANTHA: It'll be even wetter once we're in the pool.

JEREMY: Yeah. Yeah. It was a long crawl here from my little burrow, up the hill, under the Worcester monument, but now it all feels worth it.

SAMANTHA: Glad to hear it.

JEREMY: I mean, look at that moon. So bright, but not scorching like the sun. It just reaches down inside me and makes me shake, you know. Makes me feel alive.

SAMANTHA: You didn't feel alive before?

JEREMY: Alive, but not lively. Sluggish, in the slow sense, not the yummy sense. I do love me a good slug.

SAMANTHA: Who doesn't?

JEREMY: When I saw the moon and caught the warm breeze, I said to myself, Jeremy, you need to get out from under this big slab of granite and go down to the pond, because you might meet someone. Someone special. Someone who glows, someone with spots like stars. And look what I found.

SAMANTHA: *What* you found?

JEREMY: Who. I mean, look who I found. That is what I meant. "Who not what." Who is, I mean, what is your name?

SAMANTHA: Samantha.

JEREMY: I'm Jeremy. It is an absolute pleasure to meet you, to find you, Samantha. It's a big cemetery, a whole big world, and sometimes it feels like it's just cold and dark and lonely.

SAMANTHA: That's called winter.

JEREMY: But winter is over! It's spring! And here you are, and here I am.

SAMANTHA: You have a very firm grasp of the obvious.

JEREMY: I think that's one of my strengths. One of many.

SAMANTHA: Really?

JEREMY: Sure. I work out. I eat right. I take care of myself. Check out my skin mucus—moist, right? Right?

SAMANTHA: I'll take your word for it.

JEREMY: And I am fertile. I mean, I am *loaded* with fertility. (*He approaches close to her.*) And you are shiny and spotted, and so very, very fine. (*He touches her, attempts to kiss her.*)

SAMANTHA: What are you doing?

JEREMY: I figured we'd make out a little and then do the deed.

SAMANTHA: The deed?

JEREMY: Get it on. Rock the ocean. Do the nasty. You know: mate. If, if, if, you were, say, interested.

SAMANTHA: And why are you touching me?

JEREMY: I think we've got something. A connection. I feel it. I'm here, you're here. I'm ready, you're ready.

SAMANTHA: You've never done this before.

JEREMY: Not exactly.

SAMANTHA: Not exactly?

JEREMY: But I Googled "sex" on the Internet and there were lots of examples. I have a pretty good idea how it goes.

SAMANTHA: Even if you did, which you don't, what makes you think I want to mate with you?

JEREMY: What's wrong with me?

SAMANTHA: What makes you think I want to mate with anyone?

JEREMY: You've crawled all the way to Consecration Dell under the spring full moon. Why else would you be here?

SAMANTHA: Maybe I shouldn't have.

JEREMY: No, don't say that.

SAMANTHA: Maybe I should have stayed home and eaten grubs.

JEREMY: But you didn't.

SAMANTHA: Maybe I was lonely, and I just wanted to see another salamander's face.

JEREMY: Here I am. Is it such a bad face?

(She gives him a long look.)

SAMANTHA: No. Not so bad.

JEREMY: Neither is yours.

SAMANTHA: But you didn't come here for me. You just want to breed.

JEREMY: Well, yeah. But now that I've met you, it's not just random perpetuation of the species. I mean, you are stubborn and fierce, and you've got that little bump on your nose, and that spot over your left eye. You are not just some random salamander, you are Samantha. You are unique. You will be the mother of a hundred babies. I want them to be *our* babies.

SAMANTHA: You're getting better at this.

JEREMY: Oh, good. 'Cause I think I might explode.

SAMANTHA: But I'm not sure I'm going to lay eggs this season.

JEREMY: Oh, come on. What did I do now? I said the right things, and I really meant them. You've got my heart pumping so fast, it's making me dizzy.

SAMANTHA: It's not you. It's the world. I'm not sure it's fair to bring babies into this world.

JEREMY: We can try.

SAMANTHA: I did it two years ago. A couple hundred of them. It's taken me this long to recover. The father was just another guy, not so different from you.

JEREMY: But not as handsome.

SAMANTHA: No, he wasn't. But we made babies. They were so tiny and cute. And then the dragonfly larvae and the diving beetles ate most of them. One by one, picking them off. And then it got hot, remember that long heat wave that just wouldn't quit?

JEREMY: I thought I was going to cook in my own skin. I found a log and burrowed down as deep as I could.

SAMANTHA: The pond dried up early, because of the heat. The babies couldn't handle it. They had no way to escape. We lost them all, every single one. The world is getting warmer, scarier, and I don't know what to do.

JEREMY: It wasn't your fault.

SAMANTHA: No, it wasn't. But it still hurt. And I don't know how to change things.

JEREMY: I don't know either. You're right. It's a big scary world, and a lot of the time, especially lately, it feels like we lose more than we win. But we have to try.

SAMANTHA: I don't know if I'm up to it.

JEREMY: If we don't, the world will just keep getting lonelier and lonelier, until poof, one day, it's just you, or just me, and then not even that. The world will keep on going without spotted salamanders.

SAMANTHA: We're doomed.

JEREMY: Maybe. Or maybe someone, somewhere, somehow, will work to make things better. And if that happens, I want to know that I did my part, my small (but orgasmic) part. But I can't do it without you, Samantha. It takes two of us.

(SAMANTHA *thinks for a long time.* JEREMY *looks like he might explode, but he keeps it together.*)

SAMANTHA: Okay.

JEREMY: YES!

(*He touches her, tries to kiss her again. This time they do kiss.*)

SAMANTHA: Um, what are you doing?

JEREMY: You didn't like it?

SAMANTHA: I did. But you know that's not how it works, right?

JEREMY: From the videos, it looked like . . .

SAMANTHA: Porn is not an instruction manual, Jeremy. For salamanders, it works a little differently.

JEREMY: Okay.

SAMANTHA: We're going to go into the water.

JEREMY: Just so you know, there's already some guys in there.

SAMANTHA: That's good. Once we get there, we're all going to swim around. Some of the others are going to put on a show, as we are all swirling and swimming, but I'm sure none will have your moves.

JEREMY: Right. I am all about the moves.

SAMANTHA: And when we're done with the spinning liebespiel dance, you get to release your spermatophore.

JEREMY: Oh, thank God.

SAMANTHA: So will the others. And I will pick one that I will use to fertilize my eggs, before I lay them.

JEREMY: You'll know which one's mine, right?

SAMANTHA: I'm sure I will.

JEREMY: (*Under his breath.*) Pick me.

SAMANTHA: In a few days, I'll lay my eggs. And try to be a mom, all over again. Maybe you'll be a dad.

JEREMY: Oh, yeah. I can do it, I can do it, I can do it.

   (*SAMANTHA extends her hand.*)

SAMANTHA: Shall we go dance? And then, after, how about we go grab some worms?

JEREMY: Yes. Please.

SAMANTHA: It's a date.

   (*They enter the pond.*)

END OF PLAY

I SAW THIS IN PADUCAH!

by Rich Espey

I Saw This in Paducah! premiered at The Fells Point Corner Theatre's 7th Annual 10 × 10 × 10 Festival in Baltimore, Maryland, May 24–June 16, 2019.

The festival was produced by Barbara Madison Hauck (missmadasthesun @gmail.com).

The play was directed by Matthew Shea and featured the following actors:

ALICE: Jennifer Danielle Alexander
BARB: Jennifer Skarzinski
OFFSTAGE ANNOUNCER: Rob Vary
VOICE OF HARRIET TUBMAN: Shamire Casselle

CHARACTERS

ALICE, female, white, 42.
BARB, female, white, 44.
OFFSTAGE ANNOUNCER, any gender, race, age.
VOICE OF HARRIET TUBMAN, female, African American, adult.

TIME

An evening during the present time.

SETTING

A small community theater in Amarillo, Texas.

• • •

ALICE and BARB are seated in a theater.

ALICE: I just love having a friend who enjoys going to ten-minute play festivals as much as I do.

BARB: Me too! I'm never bored!

ALICE: By me?

BARB: By the plays! Even if you hate what's on stage, it's only ten minutes . . .

ALICE: Or you might love it . . .

BARB: But either way, it's over just like that!

ALICE: Right! And then on to the next!

BARB: And if something disturbs you or challenges you too much, you are not forced to think about it for more than ten minutes.

ALICE: But you can think about it afterwards.

BARB: But you don't HAVE to.

ALICE: Sometimes I like to!

BARB: And you never have to see those disturbing images again. Or feel those horrible feelings!

ALICE: Aren't there plays you WANT to see again?

BARB: It's a mute point, since we only go to WORLD PREMIERES!

ALICE: It's a *moot* point.

BARB: RIGHT!

ALICE: I love how homespun and unpretentious these festivals are.

BARB: So not like "the theeeee-uhh-tahhh."

ALICE: I know, right? Just Mom and Pop.

BARB: Not even! Mostly Mom OR Pop! Just a few martyrs keeping a 2,500-year-old art form breathing.

ALICE: Remember that festival we saw where the only prop could be a pink scarf?

BARB: Right! Because the only thing the producer owned that they could part with was a pink scarf.

ALICE: Right! They were so poor they had nothing else. The theater was so cold . . .

BARB: NO! It was so HOT! That was the Charlotte Ten By Nine By Eight by Fourteen in August!

ALICE: Oh, right! NO air conditioning. What was the cold one?

BARB: The cold one was in Grand Rapids in February. The BRRRRRRRRRR Festival!

ALICE: Right! The theater was so poor they had no heat.

BARB: No, they had heat. But the plays had to feature a snowball.

ALICE: Right! Which had to stay intact through all ten plays.

BARB: So no heat in the theater! That was tense! Since the audience's body heat threatened to melt the snowball!

ALICE: It was tense! That one had the play about the white police officer who shot the young . . .

BARB: Don't bring that up!

ALICE: The kid had thrown a snowball, and the officer overreacted, and . . .

BARB: I remember, and I don't want to think about that one anymore.

ALICE: I think about it. Every time there's another news story about a person who gets . . .

BARB: I prefer to live in the moment, Alice. Savor the ten minutes you're in.

ALICE: But Barb, what's the point if you can't recollect?

BARB: I recollect that I did most of the driving to Grand Rapids.

ALICE: Because I had just driven the weekend before to Schenectady. Right?

BARB: Right.

ALICE: What was the one in Schenectady called? That was a cold one, too.

BARB: That was the theater too poor to have heat.

ALICE: Right! Where you had to bring your own blanket . . .

BARB: And the audience had to take turns warming up the actors between plays.

ALICE: That was fun. That lovely young man . . . mmmmm . . . He was the young professor in that play about the college student whose professor assumes that because she's African Amer . . .

BARB: There's no point in rehashing that play. Or any play that we've already seen already.

ALICE: It got me thinking about how often people pre-judge, or even how I pre-judge people based on . . .

BARB: Some people brought comfortables instead of blankets. Which was wrong!

ALICE: They brought *comforters*.

BARB: Right! And we didn't even see Opening Night. We didn't even see opening weekend.

ALICE: I couldn't help getting the norovirus!

BARB: I'm not blaming you for that! It just would have been nice to have seen the candle.

ALICE: Right! It was the "Blanket and Candle" Plays.

BARB: Well, the candle was there for the first weekend. But they were so poor they didn't even have a real candle for the second weekend. They did our weekend with a paper candle.

ALICE: Right! They burned it all up.

BARB: They burned it DOWN.

ALICE: A candle burns UP.

BARB: A candle burns DOWN!

ALICE: I couldn't help getting the norovirus!

BARB: I am not driving the whole nineteen hours back home!

ALICE: This evening should be good. "The Twenty Dollar Bill Plays."

BARB: That's a boring title.

ALICE: She says after a nineteen-hour drive. (*Reading from the program.*) "Each play features a twenty dollar bill, in some meaningful way."

BARB: At least this theater has twenty dollars to spend on a prop! Unless it's counterpunch.

ALICE: *Counterfeit.*

BARB: You look just like you did before the norovirus struck.

ALICE: What's the first play called?

BARB: "Andrew and Harriet."

ALICE: Ooh . . . I bet that's going to be about Andrew Jackson and Harriet Tubman. Because he's on the twenty-dollar bill and she's supposed to replace him.

BARB: WAIT!

ALICE: What?

BARB: I saw this in Paducah!

ALICE: Paducah?

BARB: At the ten-by-nine-by-three-by-two-by-four.

ALICE: I didn't go to that.

BARB: Because you objected to the concept. Ten plays, nine minutes, three actors, and a single two-by-four for the entire set.

ALICE: I can't be moved by a piece of wood.

BARB: And I had to eat at the Denny's in downtown Paducah all by myself.

ALICE: But you got to eat the whole banana split, so . . .

BARB: And then I went, sated, to the Paducah Playhouse and saw, among other things . . . ANDREW AND HARRIET!

ALICE: Did you like it?

BARB: Doesn't matter! The rules of this contest are WORLD PREMIERES! One of these ten plays is not a world premiere!!

ALICE: But did you like it? I mean, that was Paducah. But this . . . THIS is AMARILLO!

BARB: Paducah and Amarillo are in the same WORLD . . .

ALICE: I know, but how many people . . .

BARB: Rules matter!

ALICE: But how many people were at the show in Paducah?

BARB: That's not the point.

ALICE: I know, but it'll be the first time I've seen it, and if it's a good play . . . is it a good play?

BARB: It's STALE!

ALICE: How can it be stale?

BARB: Because it's been done! Old. Passé. Viejo. You would share my outrage had you come to Paducah!

ALICE: I couldn't bear the concept of a single two-by-four!

BARB: It had a beautiful grain!

OFFSTAGE ANNOUNCER: Ladies and Gentleman, welcome to Amarillo Little Theater's Annual Festival of Ranchy Raunchy Shorts by Eight by Ten! First off is "Andrew and Harriet" by Rich Espey of Baltimore, Maryland.

ALICE: Oh, I think we saw a show by him in Ypsilanti? And maybe Albuquerque, too?

BARB: Stop the show! STOP THE SHOW! I saw this play in Paducah two weeks ago! This is NOT a World Premiere, and you promised that every show we would be seeing tonight is a World Premiere!

OFFSTAGE ANNOUNCER: You saw this two weeks ago?

BARB: In Paducah!

OFFSTAGE ANNOUNCER: What's it about?

BARB: What's it about?

OFFSTAGE ANNOUNCER: Yeah, if you saw it.

BARB: It's about Harriet Tubman confronting Andrew Jackson and explaining how she deserves to be on the twenty-dollar bill.

ALICE: Ooh, that sounds thought-provoking!

OFFSTAGE ANNOUNCER: Yeah, it's good. True, not a typical curtain-raiser, but . . .

BARB: I don't want to see it again! Harriet Tubman arguing that she deserves to be on the twenty-dollar bill because Andrew Jackson was a ringleader of American violence and racism that legally sanctioned enslavement, torture, and genocide against communities of color, and claiming that same oppression persists to this day in the form of economic inequality in which white people have a three hundred year head start at wealth building, while people of color continue to pay the literal price for those centuries of disadvantage. Ugh!

ALICE: So Harriet Tubman replacing Andrew Jackson, while far from literal monetary reparations, would at least be a symbolic first step?

BARB: I've already had to sit through this diatribe once. Rich Espey has already had his say, and now he has tried to pull one over on you! Did you even Google? Did you? Announcer?

OFFSTAGE ANNOUNCER: We . . . we did Google. And it hadn't been performed when we accepted it.

BARB: But it WAS performed. In Paducah!

OFFSTAGE ANNOUNCER: We know. He emailed us and let us know. But we already cast it, and the cast was enjoying rehearsing it, and . . .

BARB: I've seen this!

ALICE: It sounds like something people should see. Right? Right? Right?

BARB: A hundred and sixty-four people saw it in Paducah two weeks ago!

OFFSTAGE ANNOUNCER: And we want people to see it in Amarillo.

BARB: Then I am leaving!

ALICE: What is so hard about listening to the truth for ten minutes about how the United States of America was founded on violence and racism which perpetuates today and continues to enrich white people and oppress people of color?

(Long pause.)

BARB: It's the principle of the thing. World. Premieres. Only. I'll be at Denny's. Eating a banana split.

ALICE: I'm sorry about that. She's very particular, especially when it comes to ten-minute play festivals. We both are, actually. And, honestly, they really should be World Premieres if you say they're World Premieres. Rules matter. They count for something. We need order. We need things in their proper place. We need things to be as they always have been. There's too much challenging of things going on! All the hashtags and whatnot. I say . . . I say . . . Hashtag Rules And Order. Hashtag RULES AND ORDER! Right? Right???

OFFSTAGE ANNOUNCER: Are you going to leave, too? Because we are going to start.

(ALICE leaves her seat and begins to exit.)

ALICE: I'm going . . . Is it a good play? Is it?

OFFSTAGE ANNOUNCER: "Andrew and Harriet" by Rich Espey.

(Images of Andrew Jackson and Harriet Tubman are displayed. The audience can see them for a full minute, in silence.)

Voice of HARRIET TUBMAN: Every great dream begins with a dreamer. Always remember, you have within you the strength, the patience, and the passion to reach for the stars to change the world.

(ALICE returns to her seat.)

END OF PLAY

INCIDENT ON THE GOLDEN GATE BRIDGE

by David MacGregor

Original production by
Tipping Point Theatre, Northville, Michigan
Sandbox Play Festival
Produced by James Kuhl, Artistic Director (james@tippingpointtheatre.com)
October 13–14, 2019

Directed by Tyler Calhoun

Cast:
CARY: Richard Payton
NIKO: John Kent Etheridge II
JESSIE: Jaclyn Cherry

CHARACTERS

CARY, man in his 20s–30s.
NIKO, man in his 20s–40s.
JESSIE, woman in her 20s–40s.

SETTING

The Golden Gate Bridge, 220 feet above San Francisco Bay.

TIME

Now and then.

• • •

Lights up on CARY, standing on a ledge, holding onto a pole or support of some kind, and looking downward. NIKO enters, tapping at his phone. He walks past CARY, then double-takes in alarm and stops.

NIKO: Hey whoa! What's going on? Everything okay?

CARY: I'm fine.

NIKO: You sure about that?

CARY: I'm fine. Really.

NIKO: You're standing on a ledge two hundred feet above the water.

CARY: Yeah.

NIKO: Any particular reason?

CARY: Just thinking about things.

NIKO: Okay . . . what kind of things?

CARY: Everything.

NIKO: Sure. I get you. But maybe you should do that in a coffee shop or something.

CARY: I'm good.

NIKO: See, the thing is, with you hanging out there like that over the water, it kind of looks like you're maybe thinking of jumping.

CARY: I just need some perspective. And if I was in a coffee shop there would be all kinds of distractions. The noise, other people . . . but here, it's just me and the water. It kind of helps clarify things.

(*JESSIE enters, on her phone. She glances at CARY and jolts.*)

JESSIE: OH MY GOD!!! Don't do it!

(*She moves toward CARY and he quickly adjusts his position, standing on one leg.*)

NIKO: (*To JESSIE.*) Stop! Don't move! I'm talking to the man here!

JESSIE: He's going to jump! He's going to kill himself!

NIKO: He's thinking about things, okay? That's all!

JESSIE: (*Whispering intensely to NIKO.*) Are you insane? Look at him! He's going to jump! People do that here! Thirty people killed themselves jumping off this bridge last year!

NIKO: (*Right in JESSIE's face.*) I'm talking to him. We're talking, not jumping. Got it?

JESSIE: You're talking.

NIKO: That's right.

JESSIE: Talking is good.

NIKO: Yes, it is. (*Turning to CARY.*) Now listen . . . I'm not sure I caught your name.

CARY: Cary.

NIKO: Cary. Great. I'm Niko. And this is . . . ? (*He turns to JESSIE.*)

JESSIE: Jessie! My name's Jessie.

NIKO: All right then. So Cary, what exactly is on your mind? What are you trying to get perspective on?

CARY: My life, I suppose.

NIKO: Yeah?

CARY: It's not . . . not where I thought it would be.

NIKO: Hey, that happens. I mean, when you're growing up, you're going to be all kinds of things, really cool things, but then adulthood hits and . . .

JESSIE: You are totally fucked right up the ass. (*Off NIKO's look.*) Sorry. It just slipped out.

CARY: No, you're right. That's what happens. That's exactly what happens. I mean, I tried to be sensible about things. I did. And it's not like I had crazy dreams or anything. I listened to my high school counselor and took all these computer coding classes because, you know, that's where the jobs are, right?

NIKO: Sure. It's all computers these days.

CARY: And I got a job too. A good one. At Neptune Microsystems.

JESSIE: Oh, they have the coolest building downtown! The one that looks like a wave?

CARY: That's it.

NIKO: Well, that sounds pretty sweet. You still work there?

CARY: Kind of.

NIKO: Kind of what?

CARY: As it turned out, they decided to cut costs by outsourcing a lot of their coding work, so my position got eliminated. But they offered me another job in the company.

JESSIE: I've heard they're a great outfit! They even have free M&M'S in the break room!

CARY: Yeah. Cashews and espresso too. They have the Holy Trinity of Software Development pretty well covered: sugar, salt, and caffeine. I'm telling you, some of those people, you slap a two liter of Mountain Dew on their desk and they'll work for six hours straight without even looking up.

NIKO: Uh-huh. So, if you're not coding anymore, what kind of job are you doing now?

(CARY lets out a stifled sob and adjusts his feet, looking down at the water.)

NIKO:	JESSIE:
No!	No, no, no!
Don't do that!	Come back this way!
Do not look down!	Look at us! Look at us!

(CARY turns his head to NIKO and JESSIE.)

NIKO: There we are! That's it . . .

JESSIE: That is totally it. Not jumping is totally it . . .

CARY: I can't . . . I'm too ashamed to tell you what I do. And how pathetic is that? No one knows what I do. Not my friends, not my family. No one.

JESSIE: But you're still at Neptune Microsystems? (*Off CARY's nod.*) So it's still computers?

CARY: (*Shaking his head.*) No. It's . . .

NIKO: You can tell us. I mean, we're not your friends or family. We're complete strangers, so we're not going to be judging, all right? So, what do you do there?

CARY: The guy . . . CEO, owner, whatever. The guy who started the company. He's pretty well off.

JESSIE: Well, duh! He's like a multi-billionaire! He owns islands and shit.

CARY: Yeah. So, he's got this big-ass yacht. And on the deck he has a full-size basketball court so he can play basketball with his buddies. And . . . it's a yacht. A boat. On the ocean. So, once in a while a basketball will go over the side and into the water.

NIKO: Yeah?

CARY: That's my job.

JESSIE: What?

CARY: I follow behind the yacht in a powerboat . . . picking up basketballs that fall into the water. That, apparently, is what I was put on this Earth to do.

NIKO: Okay . . . wow. That does sound a little . . . I'm starting to get the whole why you need perspective thing. But hey, at least they can't outsource that job, right?

CARY: I guess. What do you do, Niko?

NIKO: Me? Oh . . . I'm a musician.

CARY: Good for you. Now see, that's a great profession. That's what I wish I had. Something creative, something . . .

NIKO: No, you don't.

CARY: What do you mean?

NIKO: It's not what you think, all right? I mean, I tell people that I'm a session player, that I get hired for various albums and concerts, but . . .

CARY: Yeah?

NIKO: Have you guys ever watched the cooking shows they have on TV?

CARY: Sometimes.

JESSIE: I love those shows! Especially when I'm just eating some pasta out of a can or something. It makes the food taste better.

NIKO: Right, well, a lot of those shows have music in the background, like when the host is about to eat some ribs at a BBQ shack or an elephant ear at a carnival. That's me. I'm the one playing the guitar or banjo or whatever. Fifteen years of lessons and practicing four hours every day and that's me. Because people don't want to listen to live music anymore. They don't want to hear real musicians who can actually play an instrument. They want some kind of synthesized, auto-tuned bullshit they can rip off the internet for free.

CARY: I don't think I ever noticed the music on those shows.

(NIKO stifles a sob, then climbs up next to CARY.)

Hey, hey, hey!

NIKO: (*Looking down.*) Whoa daddy! Oh my God, that is a long way down. I think that's enough perspective for me. (*Gingerly, he gets off the ledge.*)

JESSIE: What are you doing?

NIKO: Just . . . I'm going to need a second.

JESSIE: You could have saved him! You were up there!

NIKO: Yeah? Then you get up there with him. (*Beat.*) And what do you do, anyway?

(Long beat as CARY and NIKO look at JESSIE.)

JESSIE: I'm . . . a dog walker. Which I shouldn't be, because I have a bachelor's degree in psychology and a master's in social work, but that's what I do. I walk other people's dogs and pick up their poop. And it's a lot of poop, believe me. The dogs save it up for their walks, you know.

NIKO: Sure.

CARY: That makes sense.

NIKO: So, the social work thing . . . you couldn't get a job?

JESSIE: Are you kidding me? No, it's a booming field . . . everyone's lives are so fucked up these days, right? Well, except for the people with yachts, I guess.

CARY: Then why . . . ?

JESSIE: It's too sad. You wouldn't believe it. There's so much anger in people, so much hopelessness. I thought I could handle it . . . distance myself . . . but you see what happens to people when they lose a job . . . when they can't afford their medical bills . . . when a kid gets hooked on opiates . . . plus, I really like dogs. And hey, nobody's outsourcing picking up dog poop. That's some serious job security right there.

CARY: Listen, I appreciate you guys telling me about your lives, but you don't need to be here.

JESSIE: I'm not leaving. And if you jump, I swear to God . . . you can't.

NIKO: You really can't. Seriously. Come on down off of there.

CARY: Have you heard anything I said? I fish basketballs out of the Pacific Ocean with a net behind a five-hundred-foot yacht! That's how I make a living! There is something seriously fucked up about that!

NIKO: Absolutely there is. That is completely fucked. But it's not you.

JESSIE: Exactly! You are not the fucked up part in that equation.

NIKO: It's the times . . . the whole fucked up system. Everything is being outsourced and automated to make more money, but only for the people at the top. Your company? Neptune Microsystems with the multi-billionaire owner? I read the other day I pay more taxes than they do. It's just bullshit.

JESSIE: That's exactly what it is! Plus, we have a government basically run on bribes, which the lying sonofabitches call "lobbying," and the media just want to keep everyone pissed off at each another to boost their ratings. Do you know what we're living in? A society run by sociopaths! Our problem? I'll tell you what our problem is. We're not one of them! So we look around at the world and it just seems insane!

(Beat as CARY and NIKO stare at her.)

Dog walking gives you a lot of time to think about things.

(*NIKO and JESSIE move closer to CARY, holding their hands out.*)

NIKO: So, come on now . . .

JESSIE: Just take our hands . . .

CARY: Why are you doing this? Why can't you just leave me alone?

JESSIE: Because you're not.

(*JESSIE and NIKO keep holding their hands out, but take each other's free hand.*)

NIKO: Yeah. What she said. That perspective you're looking for? It's not down there in the water. It's right here looking back at you.

JESSIE: Absolutely. What he said.

CARY: But . . .

NIKO: Listen, I don't know you, all right? I pretty much almost walked right past you because I had my face buried in my phone.

JESSIE: Same here.

NIKO: But I do know this. If you jump it will break my fucking heart.

JESSIE: Seriously.

CARY: Why?

NIKO: That's a good question. Because honestly, if I wasn't here right now and I read about you jumping on my news feed tomorrow, I wouldn't think twice about it. I'd take another sip of coffee and check out the weather or the latest dumb-ass thing somebody said on Twitter.

JESSIE: But this is different. You're not just a name on the news. You're right here. Right now. Same as us.

NIKO: And let me ask you something. If our positions were reversed, if I got sick and tired of laying down blues riffs to back up some celebrity chef shoving brisket down his throat, or if Jessie got sick and tired of picking up other people's dog shit, would you want to see us jump?

CARY: No, of course not. That would be horrible. You guys seem really nice.

NIKO: Yeah . . . and so do you. So, come on.

JESSIE: Please . . . please.

(Long beat, then CARY takes each of their hands in his and comes down off the ledge. They all continue to hold hands as they take a moment.)

CARY: They say it's the moment you jump that you wish you hadn't.

JESSIE: I've heard that.

CARY: It's not . . . I'm not crazy. I'm just trying to understand things.

NIKO: Aren't we all . . .

(Lights fade with the trio not letting go of one another.)

END OF PLAY

OXYCONTIN FOLLIES

by *Steve Gold*

The play was produced as part of the Secret Theatre Short Play Festival (Program A) in Long Island City, Queens, New York. The festival ran from July 10 to August 24, 2019.

Cast: Victoria Gruenberg and Franco Martinez

Director: Abby Dias

CHARACTERS

GINGER, early 20s, pharmaceuticals saleswoman.
BILL VAN ZANDT, 40, a physician.

TIME

1998.

SETTING

West Virginia.

Note

No particular ethnic or racial type is specified for the characters.

• • •

A darkened stage. A woman in her early twenties is stage right, well dressed and very enthusiastic. Her name is GINGER; she is carrying a small knapsack. Stage left is a man dressed in business attire and wearing a white lab coat: Dr. BILL VAN ZANDT, about forty, low-key and amiable. It is the year 1998. The place is West Virginia.

GINGER: (*Goes to him.*) Hi! My name is Ginger.

BILL: Hello, Ginger.

GINGER: (*Shaking his hand.*) Isn't it a *beautiful* day?

BILL: Yes, indeed.

GINGER: I prefer warm weather myself—I'm from Florida. Newly arrived here.

BILL: Welcome to West Virginia. My secretary said you're with Perdue Pharma.

GINGER: Yes, I am.

BILL: How long have you been with them?

GINGER: I started three weeks ago.

BILL: How do you like it?

GINGER: Oh, it's *fabulous*!

BILL: Really.

GINGER: The possibilities are endless.

BILL: You get a commission?

GINGER: Oh, yes. And a regular salary, and a bonus. It's really terrific.

BILL: Glad to hear it.

GINGER: Perdue Pharma is a top-notch place to work. They have motivational seminars for us.

BILL: Do they?

GINGER: Yes.

BILL: Well, you seem to be very motivated.

GINGER: And they have retreats.

BILL: Retreats?

GINGER: And they pay for it, too—isn't that fabulous?

BILL: Sounds good to me.

GINGER: They have all these wonderful products. (*A bit sheepish.*) . . . And that's what I've come to talk to you about.

BILL: (*Mildly amused.*) Somehow, I suspected as much.

GINGER: You don't mind?

BILL: Not at all.

GINGER: I mean, I'm kind of new at this.

BILL: I kind of guessed that.

GINGER: I graduated college only a few months ago. And I've got a load of student loans to pay off.

BILL: (*Wryly.*) Tell me about it.

GINGER: This is my first job.

BILL: Very first job?

GINGER: That's right. So if I do or say something to make you mad . . .

BILL: Don't worry about that.

GINGER: Okay, great. Now, I came to tell you about a *fabulous* opportunity.

BILL: What's that?

GINGER: Well I'll tell you: My company, Perdue Pharma, makes a product that will change the way we think about pain management.

BILL: That would certainly be good thing . . .

GINGER: And profitable.

BILL: That too.

GINGER: Why not? Do we have to apologize for trying to make a buck?

BILL: Of course not.

GINGER: I mean, I've got student loans to pay off. Anyway, Perdue Pharma has this medication that does wonders where pain management is concerned.

BILL: What's the name of the drug?

(Pause.)

GINGER: (*Melodramatically.*) OxyContin.

BILL: OxyContin.

GINGER: OxyContin.

BILL: I only vaguely remember my pharmacology class, but isn't OxyContin given only to cancer patients, to lessen their pain?

GINGER: That was the original function. But Perdue Pharma and I believe that OxyContin can be used with other types of chronic pain.

BILL: What other types? Did they do anything to alter the formula?

GINGER: I'm not sure. I'm really terrible when it comes to chemistry. But I can get back to you on that.

BILL: Great.

GINGER: But the point is, you don't have to have cancer to see the marvelous benefits of OxyContin. If someone comes into your office with severe back pain, this drug will help them immeasurably.

BILL: Perhaps.

GINGER: No perhaps about it.

BILL: Have you got any literature I could look at?

GINGER: A*bsolutely.* (*Removes some paraphernalia from her knapsack, goes to him and hands it to him; he looks it over.*)

BILL: Hmmmm. Interesting.

GINGER: It's more than that: It's *fabulous*.

BILL: Maybe.

GINGER: You'll be even more impressed when you read all of it. I know I was.

BILL: I can see that.

GINGER: And like I said, I don't know the first thing about chemistry. So if someone like me is impressed, then someone like you—who knows more than I do—will *really* be bowled over.

BILL: I'm a family doctor, not a pharmacologist.

GINGER: But nevertheless, you do appreciate the fact that pain has been undertreated for far too long.

BILL: Has it?

GINGER: Of course it has. Survey after survey has shown that. We have to think of patients as health consumers. We have to give them what they want. I don't see anything wrong with that.

BILL: (*Puts the paraphernalia in his side pocket.*) Well, every patient is different, you know.

GINGER: That's true, and I'm not trying to tell you how to practice medicine.

BILL: I realize that . . .

GINGER: But we now have the chance to alleviate the misery of countless people. We are performing a humanitarian service. Quite frankly, I am awed to be a part of this endeavor.

BILL: Humanitarian service?

GINGER: Absolutely . . . after if we can make a few bucks on the side, that's okay, too. Here, here's a sample supply. (*Removes a bottle of pills from her knapsack, hands it to him.*)

BILL: What's the dosage?

GINGER: They're eighty-milligram tablets.

BILL: Seems a bit high.

GINGER: They didn't just pick that number out of a hat. They did lots of clinical work on this and the number they came up with is eighty milligrams. Take one of these for back pain, and you can run a marathon.

BILL: My patients have lower expectations.

GINGER: Do you have children?

BILL: Yes, I do.

GINGER: If, God forbid, one of them suffers a serious accident and requires pain medication, you won't find any better medication than OxyContin. And you know, this may sound crazy, but I almost wish I have such an accident so that I can have the opportunity to take OxyContin. That's how much faith I have in it.

BILL: What's the rate of addiction?

GINGER: How's that?

BILL: The rate of addiction.

GINGER: Oh, that? It's less than one percent.

BILL: Less than one percent?

GINGER: It says so in the material I gave you.

BILL: I'll look it over.

GINGER: Believe me, you don't have to worry about addiction. It's so safe, like taking M&M'S.

BILL: M&M'S?

GINGER: You've eaten M&M'S, haven't you?

BILL: Yes.

GINGER: What could be more safe than that?

BILL: You tell me.

GINGER: Nothing. And nothing is more safe than OxyContin, the company guarantees it.

BILL: They do?

GINGER: And I guarantee it. Look, I would never, never sell something that could have the slightest chance of doing harm to anyone. And your patients will bless the ground you walk on.

BILL: That's not why I got into medicine.

GINGER: No, of course not. (*Pause.*) Then . . . I can . . . you'll consider prescribing OxyContin?

(*Pause.*)

BILL: I can't give you a quick answer one way or the other.

GINGER: I'm not asking for one. Just keep an open mind. That's all I ask.

BILL: I will. And I'll read all the material you gave me. It's still FDA approved?

GINGER: Absolutely. I wouldn't be here otherwise. In the meantime . . . can I order you . . . a sample supply?

(*Long pause.*)

BILL: . . . Go ahead.

GINGER: (*Beaming.*) *Fabulous*!

END OF PLAY

PUTT-PUTT

by George Sapio

Originally produced in Ithaca, New York, by Bad Dog! Productions, with the following cast:

JEFF: Eric Hambury
BRIAN: A. J. Sage
DEBRA: Sylvie Yntema
DEXTER: Tim Perry

Directed by Camilla Schade

CHARACTERS

JEFF, male, 20s, exuberant.
BRIAN, male, 30s.
DEBRA, female, 30s.
DEXTER, male, 40s+.

SETTING

Office of an advertising agency. Three desks and chairs.

TIME

Current.

• • •

An office. BRIAN enters, followed by DEBRA. They are both in a state of shock. JEFF enters energetically.

JEFF: Wow! What a reaction! Did you see their faces? They were stunned! I mean I didn't think it would go over that well. Hey, look at you guys— stunned! I knew when I thought of this I was on to something. I mean is this gonna fly or is it gonna fly?

> *(He makes an airplane sound, very enthusiastic. He continues to do so, moving around the office, his arms spread out like wings. DEBRA stands, grabs his tie.)*

DEBRA: If you don't shut up I'm going to tear your face off.

JEFF: What? (*Beat.*) Oh, I get it. You're jealous!

DEBRA: Jealous?

JEFF: I don't believe it! I thought we shared everything here. A success for one of us is a success for all of us! I included you guys in the presentation— you heard me. I wasn't going to hog the glory.

DEBRA: "Glory."

JEFF: Yeah! Come on, guys. One for all, all for one?

BRIAN: Great. So it'll only take one of us to pick up all three unemployment checks.

JEFF: What?

DEBRA: What possessed you?

JEFF: I don't know! Something . . . unbelievable. I was up all night trying to think of something really . . . dynamic . . . bold . . . blockbusting! And then it hit me. It was like . . . it was like . . . ummm, can you let go of my tie?

DEBRA: No. I'm still going to strangle you.

> *(BRIAN stands, crosses to DEBRA, with some effort removes her hand from JEFF's tie.)*

JEFF: What? I don't get it.

> *(BRIAN starts to explain, then gives up and exits.)*

Oh, come on! Didn't you see their faces? They couldn't believe it!

(BRIAN returns with a box. He starts clearing out his desk.)

DEBRA: Brian? What are you doing?

(BRIAN continues to load items into the box, one by one.)

JEFF: What?

DEBRA: If he says "What" again . . .

BRIAN: I won't stand in the way.

JEFF: Wait a minute, you two . . . you're not serious??

DEBRA: You tripped.

BRIAN: And fell over the chair.

DEBRA: Got tangled up in the lamp cord.

BRIAN: Panicked.

DEBRA: Strangled yourself. Shame.

(DEXTER enters.)

DEXTER: (*To JEFF.*) Are you suffering from some kind of disorder?

JEFF: What?

(DEBRA lunges at JEFF, but DEXTER steps in front of her, confronting JEFF.)

DEXTER: Are you insane?

JEFF: I'm getting the idea you don't like my pitch. None of you.

(DEXTER's cell phone rings.)

DEXTER: Yes. Yes. No, I'm . . . Absolutely. (*Hangs up.*) Save me a box. (*Exits.*)

JEFF: Can someone explain this to me?

DEBRA: Does the phrase "lynch mob" mean anything to you?

JEFF: "Lynch mob?"

DEBRA: "Drawn and quartered?"

JEFF: What?

> *(BRIAN stands, pulls out a coin, flips it. He crosses, grabs JEFF's tie and begins to strangle him.)*

BRIAN: "Bible Heaven Putt-Putt?" That's your brilliant idea?

DEBRA: "Mini Golf for the Maxi Faithful?"

BRIAN: "Eighteen holes of good ol' down home religion?"

DEBRA: "Sink one for the Big Guy?"

> *(DEXTER enters. To DEXTER.)*

Get in line.

> *(DEXTER pulls BRIAN away from JEFF.)*

DEXTER: They liked it.

> *(Silence.)*

DEBRA: Oh, crap.

BRIAN: They liked it? How? Why?

DEXTER: They're in the conference room gushing so much it's unbelievable. Ferguson, the VP from Development, is seeing stars. He's talking about nationwide expansion, but nothing north of Tennessee. Wilkinson from corporate in Detroit keeps mumbling something about a key to the executive comfort chamber. They want a full workup by Tuesday. Eighteen diagrams, all planned out. Water traps, hills, hazards, the whole bit.

JEFF: But I've got that! I've got it all! I've got water holes, obstructions, mazes, chutes, everything! (*To BRIAN.*) You ripped my tie.

DEXTER: They seem to think it's the biggest thing since doggie aspirin.

JEFF: Aha!

DEXTER: Stroke of genius, one of them said.

JEFF: Stroke? See? They have it! They have the mindset! The subliminal aspects are already working!

DEBRA: And they want us to work it up.

DEXTER: It came from this department. They think it's a group effort. Isn't it?

BRIAN/DEBRA/JEFF: No!/NO!/YES!

JEFF: Look, guys, this is hot. They want it. They waaannt it . . .

DEXTER: You guys better get working on it.

DEBRA: Where are you going?

DEXTER: I think it's time for a vacation. (*He exits.*)

JEFF: Oh, boy! I can't believe it! We're gonna kill 'em. Let's get working. Now I'm thinking eighteen holes, nine each side, we can split it between the old and new testaments . . .

(*BRIAN crosses to his desk and resumes filling his box.*)

What are you doing? They're not going to fire you!

BRIAN: I'm quitting.

DEBRA: What?

JEFF: You can't quit!

BRIAN: Watch me.

JEFF: If you quit, they'll probably fire you.

DEBRA: Brian . . .

BRIAN: Look, this is wrong.

DEBRA: Let's talk about it, okay?

BRIAN: Are you saying you agree with this?

JEFF: Sure she is! She . . .

(*DEBRA reaches out and grabs JEFF's tie.*)

DEBRA: (*To BRIAN.*) We should talk this over. You can't just walk out.

BRIAN: I can't go through with this. It's wrong.

DEBRA: I agree, but . . . it's our job . . . and I can't . . .

BRIAN: I know. It's okay. You have, well . . . a family.

DEBRA: I have six dogs and an incontinent ferret. Brian, you can't leave me here. With him.

JEFF: That's right. You can't leave. We need you!

BRIAN: I have done some dumb things in this job. I designed a campaign for puppy thongs. I collaborated on a nationwide push for broccoli-flavored JELL-O. But here I draw the line. I will not now, not ever, work on an ad campaign that features the slogan, "Stroke your putts for Jesus"!

(*He frees JEFF from DEBRA again.*)

DEBRA: Brian, I know. I do. But please think about it. I mean don't think about it. Who will care?

BRIAN: Weren't you listening in there? He wants to replace the windmill obstacle with a revolving Christ on the cross!

JEFF: Yeah, and if you hit the cross as it revolves, the eyes light up and a deep voice booms, "You're damned!"

BRIAN: Debra, do you really think this is a good idea?

DEBRA: Hell, no. But that's not what I get paid for. Wow, Brian. Nine years of working with you, and I never knew you were religious.

BRIAN: Who said I was religious?

DEBRA: I thought . . . Then what are you bitching about?

(*BRIAN digs out his wallet, pulls out a small certificate.*)

National Putt-Putt Champion?

JEFF: What?

BRIAN: Nine times. Three years in a row.

DEBRA: You're the National Putt-Putt Champion?

BRIAN: I've been playing since I was able to walk.

JEFF: Oh, wow.

(*BRIAN pulls out a photo.*)

BRIAN: That's me with my first putter. I was Idaho's youngest putt-putt professional. I have nine golden balls. That's a world record. I took the Masters at the Hawaiian Rumble Golf Course with a perfect eighteen. Which isn't easy to do with the course volcano going off every ten minutes. When that goes off, the ground shakes.

DEBRA: I think reality just bent.

JEFF: I'm in the presence of greatness! Wow! You must be a putt-putt god!

BRIAN: (*Flattered.*) Hardly a . . . I still compete, you know.

JEFF: No kidding!

BRIAN: Yep.

JEFF: I love putt-putt. My parents used to take me all the time. I haven't played in years, though.

BRIAN: It's really good for hand-eye coordination. Builds good concentration. Strengthens character. When I was young and just learning I caddied for some of the greats. They taught me everything I know.

DEBRA: Why didn't you ever tell me about this?

BRIAN: Well, I used to mention it to people, but I would get all of these weird responses. People would either look at me kinda strange, some giggled, others shunned me completely. I had to move twice.

JEFF: That's so sad.

BRIAN: But I never gave it up.

JEFF: Good for you!

BRIAN: When you find something you love, something that fills your soul, you have to stick with it. Through thick and thin. No matter what.

JEFF: Or else what are you?

BRIAN: You're nothing, that's what. Well, I better get packing.

DEBRA: Wait a minute! We've worked together nine years and you never once told me about being the god of putt-putt!

BRIAN: I know. I'm sorry.

DEBRA: Sorry? I thought we were friends! I thought we trusted each other.

BRIAN: I wasn't sure you would understand.

DEBRA: About PUTT-PUTT?!

BRIAN: Actually, the term is "alternative golf." "Putt-putt" applies only to non-professional courses. Besides, there are a lot of people who find it easy to ridicule.

DEBRA: I would never ridicule you.

BRIAN: I didn't want to take that chance. I . . . didn't want you to . . . think . . .

DEBRA: Never, Brian . . . never.

BRIAN: I've learned to be cautious. I'm going to finish packing up.

(*DEXTER enters.*)

DEBRA: I thought you were off to Disneyland.

DEXTER: (*Ignoring her.*) Rockaway Beach. 1983.

(*BRIAN freezes.*)

I knew it. As soon as you left the conference room, the veep from Pittsburgh sent out a research memo to R&D. Looking for, among other things, celebrities willing to endorse the project. And you know what they found? They found you. Brian Sanderson, three-time world champion and the youngest person ever to beat The Iron Horse.

JEFF: The Iron Horse?

BRIAN: It's the hardest alternative golf hole in the world. Some say it was designed by the devil himself. Nine levels of ramps, a dozen chutes, four rotating obstacles and a little traveling choo-choo with an empty coal car that you have to hit just right or . . .

DEXTER: Only two people have ever done it. And you were not even out of knee pants. You are our mascot. We are going to turn the putt-putt world on its ear!

JEFF: No you're not. He's quitting.

DEXTER: Quitting? You're not quitting.

BRIAN: I am.

DEXTER: You quit and you're fired!

BRIAN: I'm sorry. I can't do this. The sport means too much to me.

DEBRA: Then you should quit.

JEFF/DEXTER: WHAT?

DEXTER: (*To DEBRA.*) You're fired, too!

JEFF: Does that mean I'm head of the department?

DEXTER: Look, we need to think about this. You can't quit. We need you. Both of you.

BRIAN: Look, Dexter . . .

DEXTER: You can't leave me here with him!!

DEBRA: Cut it out! Look, the two of you . . . please leave. Let me talk to Brian.

BRIAN: Debra . . . my mind is made up . . .

DEBRA: Go! Shoo!

JEFF: Ahh, the subtle female touch . . .

(*DEXTER grabs JEFF's tie and hauls him offstage.*)

DEBRA: Brian.

BRIAN: I'm sorry.

DEBRA: So am I. I could have left a couple of times, I had a couple of really good offers . . . but I didn't. I wanted to stay with you. I even . . . named my ferret Brian.

BRIAN: The incontinent one?

DEBRA: He wasn't . . . then . . .

BRIAN: I wish I'd known . . . about the ferret, I mean . . . but this is something I have to stand by . . .

DEBRA: I understand. But you're not thinking about this the right way.

BRIAN: What do you mean?

DEBRA: This campaign could be huge, Brian.

BRIAN: I know. It will be.

DEBRA: And you won't be in it at all. Do you think they'll include you, even as the god of putt- . . . alternative golf after you quit?

BRIAN: I expect not.

DEBRA: And you'll be watching it from the outside. Watching your sport gain recognition, shaking off the putt-putt onus . . . and who will they get to be the spokesman? It won't be you.

BRIAN: No. It'll be "Hook" Harrison. From Toledo. He's a . . . a . . . a . . . ohmygod . . . he licks his putter after every hole in one!

DEBRA: That's right. It will be "Hook" Harrison. Not Brian Sanderson . . . the one person perfectly poised to take alternative golf from pathetic obscurity to the national spotlight. Not Brian Sanderson, who could have made sure the ad campaign was true to the natural integrity of his beloved legendary sport steeped in honorable tradition.

BRIAN: I didn't think . . . (*About that.*)

DEBRA: Instead this campaign's visible face will be Hook Harrison, a putter-licker from Toledo. Not the proper god of alternative golf, nine-time national champion Brian Sanderson, who missed his chance to have served as the only true spokesperson for . . . Sacred Holes Putt-Putt Paradise.

BRIAN: Did you really name the ferret after me?

DEBRA: I did. Before he developed his bladder problem. I love you, Brian.

BRIAN: I love you, Debra.

DEBRA: Shall we go make a putt-putt heaven?

BRIAN: You're right. Let's do it! (*As they exit.*) Y'know . . . I actually liked the idea where a hole in one makes the whale puke up a dancing Jonah . . .

(*Lights fade.*)

END OF PLAY

RUN. HIDE. FIGHT.

by Adrienne Dawes

RUN. HIDE. FIGHT. was originally produced by The Fire This Time Festival in New York, New York, with Cezar Williams as producer. It opened in New York City at the Kraine Theater on January 24, 2019.

Stage Management by Hanako Rodriguez and Eli Schleicher

Directed by Kevin R. Free

Cast:
SOLOWAY: Phillip Gregory Burke
WILSON: Dana Costello
BARKER: Carl Fisk

CHARACTERS

SOLOWAY, 20s–30s, M or masculine person, an eager crisis actor on his
   first day of work.
WILSON, 20s–40s, F or feminine person, an experienced crisis actor with
   fight training.
BARKER*, white, 20s–30s, M or masculine person, a disgruntled crisis
   actor, Wilson's former boyfriend.
Various voices offstage (can be prerecorded).

SETTING

Present day, United States. An office building.

CASTING/DIRECTOR'S NOTE

The character breakdown for *RUN. HIDE. FIGHT.* is intentionally open and flexible to encourage the casting of diverse performers of differing abilities, races, sizes, and gender identities. Use this opportunity to challenge the idea that a dark comedy must be populated solely with able-bodied, thin, cisgender, and heterosexual white people. Casting outreach must include actors of color, queer performers, actors with disabilities, non-binary actors, trans actors, gender non-conforming actors, and actors of all body sizes. Please advocate for this outreach to continue beyond just this one play and audition process.

*NOTE

The role of BARKER could be played entirely by an actor offstage or the script offers notes on fight choreography to share just the initial beats of a physical fight between BARKER and WILSON. There should be **no** physical violence depicted onstage.

• • •

In the dark, we hear the soft lull of telephones ringing, copiers printing, keys tapping on a keyboard. High-quality office ambiance. Suddenly the sound of a gunshot pierces the air. Screams. Lights bump to red. The crackling sound of an office paging system.

VOICE ON LOUDSPEAKER: (*Shakily.*) Dr. Red is in the lobby! I repeat: Dr. Red, lobby. We need level one responders NOW . . . !

> (*Sound of screaming, the loud speaker abruptly cuts off. SOLOWAY suddenly runs onstage, yelling. He trips and falls to the ground, very presentational.*)

SOLOWAY: Ugh. If you're going to fall, fall safe. (*He casually walks offstage. He runs in again yelling, super urgent energy. He trips and falls again, landing in an awkward pose. Sighs.*) Come on. Disney princess. (*He walks offstage again. He runs in, full speed and lands a perfect trip and fall. He begins to crawl back, whimpering.*)

I'm just a temp . . . just a temp . . . please, don't hurt me!

(The office paging system turns on again. Another voice whispers into the loudspeakers.)

VOICE ON LOUDSPEAKER 2: (*Sobbing.*) . . . there . . . cookies in the oven . . . burning! He's . . . second floor . . . this is real. It's real!

(Another scream! The loudspeaker cuts off. SOLOWAY stands up, brushing himself off. Unbothered. WILSON enters, dressed in frumpy business casual. A fresh bruise is visible under one of her eyes. Lights shift.)

WILSON: What are you doing in here?!

SOLOWAY: Oh um, I'm . . . I was just . . .

WILSON: (*Sharply.*) They called for level one responders. You're supposed to be downstairs.

SOLOWAY: I'm not a level one, I'm . . .

(WILSON reads his employee nametag from a safe distance.)

WILSON: Soloway. Temp.

SOLOWAY: Yeah. Who . . . what are you?

(He reaches for her nametag, which hangs right at her chest. She swiftly pulls away from him.)

WILSON: (*Snaps.*) Woah! Workplace Harassment Sim 232!

SOLOWAY: I don't know that one yet . . .

WILSON: It's basically: never touch your coworkers. It's a huge liability. So don't touch me . . . unless I give you my full consent.

SOLOWAY: I won't. Ever. I'm sorry—(*Tries to read her nametag.*) Ellson?

WILSON: *Wilson.* Payroll. Temps are supposed to be runners. You should be outside right now.

SOLOWAY: I know, I got all turned around . . . it's my first day. First sim.

(WILSON sighs, takes a little pity on him.)

WILSON: Well, if you're going to hide you have to help me pull these chairs against the door. Keep the lights off!

(*SOLOWAY grabs a heavy office chair and clumsily throws it at the door. WILSON hisses.*)

The Shooter's not supposed to know we're in here!

SOLOWAY: Oh. Okay.

(*They quietly stack chairs against the door.*)

WILSON: Are you lifting with your legs?

SOLOWAY: It's an *active* shooter?

WILSON: Yes?!

SOLOWAY: So, I'm probably not thinking about my back right now. I'm thinking of like survival, my family, my girlfriend! Julia, maybe Jules for short. (*Actorly, faux emotional.*)

Jules *begged* me not to take this temp job but . . .

WILSON: (*Rolls her eyes.*) Okay . . .

SOLOWAY: But I went to one of those for-profit art institutes? Total scam. $100K in loans for what? Certificate in "Psychology of Game Design." The hell am I supposed to do with that?

WILSON: I couldn't tell you . . .

SOLOWAY: *Exactly!* So, I had to take this job today. *I had to. Had to.* (*Pause, grins.*) Urgency. Stakes.

WILSON: (*Affirmative.*) Mmhmm.

(*They sit, hiding together in the darkness.*)

SOLOWAY: What's Wilson's backstory?

WILSON: Oh, Wilson's trying to not die today.

SOLOWAY: (*Frowns.*) Oh. Okay.

(*WILSON stops and looks at him.*)

WILSON: (*Sighs.*) Alright. Wilson has a . . . tramp stamp. She got it right out of accounting school. She thought she was in love . . . thought it was for real this time but . . . just another controlling, possessive asshole. Per usual . . .

SOLOWAY: What was the . . .

WILSON: *I'm getting to it.* (*Wistful, actorly.*) Wilson still has that tat, to this very day. Big block letters across her lower, *lower* back: "*Accounts Receivable.*"

SOLOWAY: (*Bursts into laughter.*) Oh my god! That's amazing! Wilson from Payroll with the dirty tattoo! Meanwhile she's dressed like . . .

WILSON: (*Frowns.*) These are my real clothes.

SOLOWAY: Oh, your real, like you wear in them in your daily life?

WILSON: They're my audition clothes.

SOLOWAY: . . . Sure. What's with your eye? (*WILSON touches her bruised eye, gently.*) That's makeup, right? The bruise?

WILSON: (*Sharply.*) Anything else you have to say about my appearance? Because we're getting *real* close to Workplace Harassment Sim 238 . . .

SOLOWAY: No, no I was . . . I just meant . . . the tattoo . . . the backstory. Such a compelling thing to play because . . . Wilson doesn't end up in Accounts Receivable.

WILSON: She's in Payroll.

SOLOWAY: (*Smiles, appreciatively.*) Wilson's in Payroll. It's . . . smart is all.

(*WILSON offers a smile. Sound of a distant scream. Gunshots.*)

How long have you been doing this?

WILSON: A few years.

SOLOWAY: *Wow.* It doesn't get . . . depressing?

WILSON: It does but . . . money's good. Steady. Every office needs the training, every hospital, church, military base . . . daycare. We do a lot of daycares, schools. I was hiding with a little girl, first grade class. She wrote "Love you Mama and Dad" on her arm in magic marker. In case they found her body.

SOLOWAY: (*Shudders.*) Jesus.

WILSON: Yeah . . . just the way the world is now. (*Pause.*) Usually Barker hides with me but . . . they probably moved him . . . (*She looks down at her watch.*)

SOLOWAY: Who's Barker?

WILSON: He's my . . . he *was* my . . . another Hider assigned to a group of clients. We usually meet up and hide out together, one big group but they probably moved him to Fighter.

SOLOWAY: Fighters fight? Like real fights?

WILSON: Like stage fighting.

SOLOWAY: Damn, do clients ever win?

WILSON: No. Clients have a lead Fighter. *He* does the fighting.

SOLOWAY: Or she.

WILSON: No, no we're simulating "real attacks." Women hide or run. Women don't fight.

SOLOWAY: *Bullshit.*

WILSON: Oh, I know! I auditioned to be a Shooter because I have all this fight training but . . .

SOLOWAY: You do?

WILSON: Yeah, they told me the Shooter is always scripted "Gunman" not "Gunwoman." Clients would never be afraid of me.

SOLOWAY: Maybe not in those pants.

(*WILSON punches him playfully, then quickly pulls away.*)

WILSON: Oh my god, I'm so sorry . . .

SOLOWAY: You didn't hurt me (much) . . .

WILSON: No. I shouldn't have put my hands on you. That's really bad . . .

SOLOWAY: It's OK. You have my consent to hit me when I'm being dumb. Just no ninja shit.

(WILSON grins. Suddenly, we hear screaming just offstage. SOLOWAY cowers.)

That sounds so real! Where are they?

(WILSON frowns, looking at her watch.)

WILSON: I don't think . . . no . . . Shooter's not supposed be up here yet.

(She crawls over to the doors and listens. WILSON suddenly gestures to SOLOWAY: DON'T MOVE!)

(Sound of quiet tapping at the door.)

BARKER: *(Offstage.)* Wilson. You there?

(WILSON gestures to SOLOWAY: DON'T SPEAK!)

BARKER: *(Offstage.)* I got separated from my group . . .

WILSON: *(Sharply.)* Then you're a runner or you're dead, Barker . . .

BARKER: *(Offstage.)* I'm not dead . . . let me in.

WILSON: You've died before. You'll die again, it's not a big . . .

BARKER: *(Offstage. Snaps.)* I'm not dying today!!! *(Calmer.)* Will you open the door? I have to talk to you. Have to talk to you now . . .

WILSON: There's nothing else to say! You put your hands on me? You hurt me?! Relationship: over. We're done!

SOLOWAY: *(Whispers, to WILSON.)* He's your . . . ?

(WILSON nods. The door shakes violently as BARKER tries to push his way in.)

BARKER: *(Offstage.)* Open this door!

WILSON: No! We're not getting into this at work! Just leave me alone!

SOLOWAY: *(Yelling.)* Yeah and there's . . . there's somebody in here!

(WILSON'S eyes widen: WHAT ARE YOU . . . ?)

BARKER: *(Offstage, yelling.)* Who's that? Who's in there?!!!

SOLOWAY: What the hell is he doing?!

(*WILSON grabs a chair and flattens herself against the wall.*)

WILSON: (*To SOLOWAY.*) We don't offer this sim. Intimate-partner violence . . .

BARKER: (*Growls.*) Who's in there!?

(*WILSON mouths to SOLOWAY: STAY DOWN! Loud gunshot. SOLOWAY drops to the ground. WILSON yells out in shock. Suddenly the door is kicked open. WILSON holds up her chair, shaking. As BARKER tries to climb inside, WILSON smashes her chair down onto his head hard. WILSON climbs through the door after him. We hear the sounds of a loud struggle: WILSON yells! A loud gunshot. Silence. Sound of heavy breathing. WILSON reenters, gun in hand. She sees SOLOWAY still curled up on the ground. She kneels down next to him, holding back tears. SOLOWAY sits up.*)

SOLOWAY: Is he . . .

(*WILSON pushes back onto her feet in shock.*)

WILSON: Oh my god! I thought . . . I thought you were dead!

SOLOWAY: I was acting. (*He slowly rises to his feet.*)

Are you . . . are you going to be . . . ?

(*WILSON nods, wiping back tears.*)

And he . . . he really . . . that was a real . . .?

(*WILSON nods.*)

Can I . . . ?

(*He holds his arms open. WILSON nods and they embrace. Sound of sirens grows loudly around them. Lights fade to black.*)

END OF PLAY

SALLY MARS' REPAIR SHOP

by Sarah Elisabeth Brown

Original production
Sally Mars' Repair Shop was presented by Squeaky Bicycle Productions
at Theatre for a New City, New York City, in an evening of short plays called,
"All Guts and Some Glory"
March 11, 2019, 7:00 p.m.

Director: Kathryn McConnell

SALLY MARS: Rose-Alma Lamoureux
ROBIN YOUNG: Robyn Michele Frank

CHARACTERS

SALLY MARS, 55, a business-minded nuts and bolts repair woman.
ROBIN YOUNG, 18, a peppy cheerleader in the midst of a deep soul crisis.

SETTING

Sally Mars' Repair Shop. Sally's office looks like any repair shop in America
with a big 70s metal desk, paperwork and a phone on it. A nude male calendar on the wall. Anywhere USA.

TIME

The present.

• • •

SALLY MARS, wearing coveralls and a tool belt, fills out paperwork while reflexively eating Cheetos from a great big metal bowl. ROBIN YOUNG enters wearing her cheerleading outfit.

ROBIN YOUNG: Um. I'm here to be repaired.

> (*SALLY jumps, Cheetos go flying. SALLY holds out a Cheeto. ROBIN simultaneously holds her hand out to shake.*)

SALLY MARS: Cheeto.

ROBIN YOUNG: Robin Young. (*She takes the Cheeto, twiddles with it awkwardly, then hides it.*)

SALLY MARS: Of course, you are. I'm Sally Mars. *The* Sally Mars.

ROBIN YOUNG: You do repairs here, right? I mean, the sign said repairs and I don't have an appliance like a vacuum or anything, but I definitely need a repair.

SALLY MARS: Have a seat, Doll. Are you a cheerleader?

ROBIN YOUNG: That's the problem! I mean it's not THE problem. It's the part that makes the problem into a problem, if you know what I mean.

SALLY MARS: Do you have a boyfriend?

ROBIN YOUNG: Gosh, it's like you can read my mind. Uggh.

SALLY MARS: Yes, but cannot tell if we are having a cheerleader problem, or a boyfriend problem. Please clarify for Sally.

ROBIN YOUNG: I'm here because I'm wicked sick and I need some serious psychoanalytic analysis.

SALLY MARS: Nah uh ah, no need for those big fancy words. I, here at "Sally Mars' Repair Shop," take a simple hammer and nail approach.

ROBIN YOUNG: I can't make myself interested in sex with my boyfriend anymore.

SALLY MARS: Now we're getting somewhere.

ROBIN YOUNG: I have these totally weird thoughts inside my head these days. Never mind. Weird. Weird, weird, weird. Okay, what?

SALLY MARS: Robin, I'm going to have to ask you a very intense and personal question.

ROBIN YOUNG: Yes, please. Good.

SALLY MARS: What happens to you during the sexual act?

ROBIN YOUNG: Oh, that's easy. It's the same every time. I lie down, he gets on top, we kiss, then he puts it in. He goes faster and faster getting really short of breath. He says, "Robin, Robin, I love you!" And then he rolls over and goes to sleep. It's pretty fun, I guess. But lately there's these other thoughts in my head that completely whack me out like . . .

SALLY MARS: And how many orgasms per sexual encounter?

ROBIN YOUNG: Um.

SALLY MARS: Is it one big one? Many little ones?

ROBIN YOUNG: Hmmm . . .

SALLY MARS: Or is it simply pleasant to be a vessel for his pleasure.

ROBIN YOUNG: Uh . . .

SALLY MARS: Preferring the pressure of the pound rather than the hurl of the climax?

ROBIN YOUNG: Well . . .

SALLY MARS: Robin, do you feel anything at all while this is happening?

ROBIN YOUNG: I DON'T FEEL ANYTHING! He says, "Does that feel good," and I say, "Yes," but I'm lying! I'm a liar!

SALLY MARS: There there, have no fear. You've come to the right place. You are exactly the sort of pupil I've devoted my life to. A perfect candidate for repair. Let's take a look at this diagram. The confusion began with Freud when he said that women outgrow clitoral stimulation as they mature, becoming satisfied only with vaginal stimulation. He put the emphasis on the hole, not the lump. We want to get back to lumps, Dear. It's lumps that count. Can you imagine a man having a sexual experience without his penis involved? Well, somehow that's what is expected of women. It's wrong, Robin, plain wrong, and I've devoted my whole life to righting that wrong. Here at Sally Mars' Repair Shop, skilled repair technicians will show you what your body is truly capable of. Because I can see that you are a plum, my dear, a plum that is hardly ripe, and I will not let you fall from the tree until you are deeply purple.

ROBIN YOUNG: I want to be purple, I do! But Sally Mars, there's more . . . I'm sick. I'm deathly ill.

SALLY MARS: Let me tell you a story, I, here at Sally Mars' Repair Shop believe in personal disclosure anecdotes as a path to a healing relationship between client and counselor. My disappointment in sex came as soon as I started having it with other people. As a child of the seventies, I was educated—perhaps overeducated—about my parts. I spent a lifetime between age nine and fourteen thinking sex would be the greatest time had by anyone alive. It's not that my first experience was bad. It happened on a waterbed in a stranger's bedroom at a high school party one week before my fifteenth birthday with a real boyfriend. In the moment of penetration, I screamed out, "This is great!" However, I was confused. This long-anticipated act had nothing to do with "The Spot." Zero. It was close, but sensation-wise in a completely different region of the body. "This can't be the 'main event' everyone talks about," I thought, "You're in the wrong spot!" But no. This. Was. It. The awful truth was that "main event" was meant to hit his spot but not mine. What an Earth-shattering disappointment. It wasn't the boyfriend I was upset with. No, I was furious with biology itself! Then, the unthinkable happened. People acted like the spot, that wasn't the spot, was actually the spot! Everywhere I turned folks talked about the man and the woman climaxing together. Movies said it, books said it, porn said it, it seemed that I was the only one who didn't say it. Well, this made me feel like one twisted sister. Hadn't I learned from my seventies education? Hadn't I done experiments on myself? Did people really think a passageway that was strong enough to stretch a human head through it was a super-sensitive-sensation factory? The "main event" was, at best, pleasant, often boring, and at worst, painful. What a con.

ROBIN YOUNG: Yes, I'm sure it is a con, but that's not quite it. See . . .

SALLY MARS: Don't worry, Doll. Out of this grew a productive passion to start Sally Mars' Repair Shop, and I am going to set up an appointment with my premiere Repair Technician, right now. Her name is Vera Venus, and she can help instruct you on the positive functional value your body has to offer.

ROBIN YOUNG: Are you saying the Repair Technician is a girl?

SALLY MARS: Vera Venus is female, yes.

ROBIN YOUNG: No no, I can't do that because I'm sick!

SALLY MARS: It can feel like an illness when there are all these orgasms inside you clambering to get out. But have no fear, we will release them from their hollow prison.

ROBIN YOUNG: No, no, you're not diagnosing me correctly.

SALLY MARS: There is only one true issue for females. Here at Sally Mars' Repair Shop, I will fix your Failure to Orgasm, I swear it.

ROBIN YOUNG: It's not about that.

SALLY MARS: This is the most important issue anyone has ever had, or ever will have!—You'll soon see what I mean.

ROBIN YOUNG: It's about the female person! No see, just let me tell you. I was with these friends of mine the other day, and we were at the sand dunes for our graduation party because we'd just finished high school. My boyfriend was there—and we all decided to . . . drop acid. I'd never done it before, but I was feeling so good about my life and my future—I've always been very popular—I remembered I had nothing to fear but fear itself, everything inside my head went calm, and I ate the paper. I never used to take risks like this. My boyfriend, Tommy, was talking about a chipmunk smoking cigarettes, and an ice cream truck with sunglasses, and we were all laughing really hard—even though it doesn't seem all that funny now— when I decided to take a walk by myself, away from the pack. I never used to take risks like this. I don't know, but can I tell you something very strange? Everywhere I looked, there were women's breasts and butts. The dunes took on a new meaning, a fleshy meaning. I looked down at the crevice in a tree stump and realized it was a vagina and I had to stroke it. Did I just say that? This is not me. I'm so embarrassed for myself—but all around me the small trees curled up like fallopian tubes and many other unnamed feminine internal organs—and I wanted to make love to them all! This was kind of a shock to me because I've always liked boys. Acid is definitely weird. There I am I reaching deep inside the sand like I was reaching towards this powerful center, like it was deep in the womb of the Earth and not God off in the sky somewhere. This happened to me two weeks ago, and since then, I haven't been able to look at a penis. I can't stop thinking about breasts. I haven't been able to eat or sleep because, oh yeah, I forgot to tell you about this part of the story, so while I was tripping for my first time and discovering I wanted to touch a vagina, on my little walk I was having by myself, I found a cave and I went in. Inside, my vision narrowed and I forgot the rest of my friends completely. It was as if I'd lived in that cave my entire life and there was nothing else but a small patch of light at the end. I knew in that moment that I was a prisoner doomed to stare forever at that light and whatever came into that opening would determine my entire future and the meaning of my entire life. I sat there, and for a time my life was nothing but a grain of sand and some sunlight. Then the real thing happened, a woman walked in with purple hair and yellow lips. It turned out to be my best friend, Chloe, but I didn't have time to ask her how she got a chance to die her hair purple in the last fifteen minutes because all I could think was, "Oh my God, Chloe has breasts!" I mean I never understood why guys liked 'em so much, but all of a sudden, I wanted to run my fingertips along the tops of 'em. Just as I was working up the courage to tell her, Tommy showed up at the end of the cave. He shooed her away, but she bit his arm! Now, Chloe never liked it that I was dating Tommy, do you think Chloe might be . . . ? Then Tommy got mad and threw me over his shoulder like I was a cave girl—which I was. He took me home, gave me some tea, and put me to bed. Of course, I couldn't think of anything other than breasts, so for lack of any others around I touched my own, and WOW! Was I impressed! I had them too, and I liked 'em. The last thing I wanted to do was lie in bed, but Tommy insisted I must be so traumatized, so all I could do was stare at the wallpaper as it changed to different patterns and different shades of yellow. As I watched this yellow wallpaper, I began to see letters on the wall that changed to numbers as I strained to see. Eventually, I was able to make out a phone number but I didn't have the guts to call it up. But then I got the guts, and it turned out to be Sally Mars' Repair Shop. I figured it was a sign, so I signed up. Gee, I have no brain! I never used to take risks and everything was fine, just fine. I was Tommy's girl and everyone liked me because of it. I was popular. I was safe. I'm so embarrassed for myself. What kind of stupid impulse led me here?

SALLY MARS: Welcome to yourself, my dear. Welcome to the world of the "True You." Let me write up your ticket. Repair number 6089742. "Failure to Orgasm brought on by a Crisis of Sexual Orientation."

ROBIN YOUNG: And Soul.

SALLY MARS: " . . . and Soul." Now, we'll have to keep you here I'm afraid. Some repairs are like that.

ROBIN YOUNG: I'm a real fixer upper, huh?

SALLY MARS: You? No, Doll. Refreshing is what you are. There's nothing about you that needs fixing except the notion that you need to be fixed— and that could take awhile.

ROBIN YOUNG: That's deep.

SALLY MARS: Is it? Anyway, we'll have to keep you in the shop for at least a month.

ROBIN YOUNG: A month? What are you going to do with me for a whole month?

SALLY MARS: Everyone wants the quick fix, the in-and-out Jiffy-Lube approach, and that IS what I aim to do more than any other repair shop you may find in your yellow pages. However, not everything can be stuck together with duct tape and crazy glue.

ROBIN YOUNG: Believe me, I know that, cause Sally Mars? There's something else I forgot to tell you.

SALLY MARS: I think we pretty much got it, Doll. Once you've had treatment, you'll say to me, "Sally Mars. It really is all about the proper climax."

ROBIN YOUNG: Is that really all it is? Because it feels so terribly wild, and vast, and unknowable.

SALLY MARS: Now, looky-look who's being deep.

ROBIN YOUNG: Because there's this other part. Once I touched Chloe's breasts, and my own breasts, and finished having thoughts about breasts, well, I realized there was something I wanted beyond the breast. Something not from this world. No, not an alien. It was something euphoric I felt out there in the dunes, something that was central to my very being. Something vaster than life itself, and eternal too. That's it! That's what I want! Sally Mars, can your repair shop help me reclaim my eternal euphoria?

(SALLY MARS rips up the work order and throws it away. She writes up a new one.)

SALLY MARS: Repair number 6089742. Wants "Failure to Orgasm due to Crisis of Sexual Orientation and Soul and Failed Quest for Eternal Euphoria."

ROBIN YOUNG: That's the diagnosis I can relate to.

SALLY MARS: I don't even know what to write anymore. Look, Doll, according to radical studies, probably done in cult-ish environments, the longest known female orgasm is fifteen minutes long—That does not count as "Eternal."

ROBIN YOUNG: It's all about my desire for eternal euphoria. I'm pretty sure it was there before I was born, and will be there after I die.

SALLY MARS: Then what the heck do you need it now for?

ROBIN YOUNG: I can't go off to college without it.

SALLY MARS: Very well. Gather your things. Wait outside that door and Vera Venus will be along to collect you and bring you to room two-eleven.

(SALLY points to a door. ROBIN turns to go.)

ROBIN YOUNG: And Sally, there's something else.

SALLY MARS: I promise you everything is about to change.

ROBIN YOUNG: Thank you. That's all I wanted to say.

SALLY MARS: All in a day's work.

(ROBIN exits.)

(Phone rings. SALLY answers.)

Sally Mars' Repair Shop. Go ahead, don't be shy, I've heard it all. Uh huh, oh you're looking for eternal euphoria too, are you? Yeah, aren't we all? I mean, as a matter of fact, I'm inventing a new program as we speak. It's on just the topic. I haven't worked out all the details yet. However, I feel certain I'll have it added to my list of purchasable repairs by next week. Yes, I agree, sex is one possible gateway to the divine. Once we clear up the rubble along the way. But then again, that's what my repair shop is all about. When would you like to come in?

END OF PLAY

SARDINES

by Mona Deutsch Miller

Sardines was first produced by Fierce Backbone at the Lounge Theatre in Hollywood, May 16–19, 2019, for the CORE Playwriting Festival 2019: 8 Original Voices Telling Authentic LA Stories.

CELIA: Stephanie Keefer
CELIA 2: Elena-Beth Kaye
BERYL: Jordan Carlson
BERYL 2: Rylee Cravens

Director: Cloe Kromwell

CHARACTERS

CELIA, 40s–50s, disheveled, dirty, with a loaded shopping cart, surrounded by bags.
CELIA 2, similar age and look, dressed in a corresponding way.
BERYL, professionally dressed, 20s–50s, organized, sympathetic, carrying a purse.
BERYL 2, Beryl's inner voice, visible only to her, similar age and look, dressed in a corresponding way.

SETTING

A sidewalk with bench, outdoors.

Time

The present.

• • •

CELIA sits on the bench by her shopping cart, loaded with bags, or surveys her stuff. Other bags are around her, some on the ground. She is wrapped in a filthy blanket that overflows away from her, and hides CELIA 2, her alter ego/inner voice, completely. BERYL approaches from offstage. She looks at CELIA. BERYL 2, dressed similarly, follows her, too closely, duplicating all her movements. BERYL does not seem to be bothered by BERYL 2, at least at first. CELIA does not react to BERYL 2, whom she cannot see. CELIA responds only to BERYL. BERYL 2 speaks only to BERYL and can only be heard by BERYL. As BERYL seems to be looking particularly sympathetically toward CELIA:

BERYL 2: There she is again. Don't give her any money.

(*BERYL nods.*)

BERYL: (To *CELIA.*) Hello. Um, would you . . . I have a package I can give you. Not money, but—could you use some socks? Hairbrush?

(*CELIA's arms fly up to her hair. CELIA's alter, CELIA 2, dressed similarly to CELIA, slides out from under the blanket but BERYL and BERYL 2 do not react. CELIA 2 speaks only to CELIA.*)

CELIA 2: Don't get mad, whatever you do. Remember to smile or you won't get any stuff.

CELIA: (*To BERYL.*) What's wrong with my hair?

CELIA 2: Oh boy.

BERYL: Uh, nothing.

CELIA: Sorry. Sorry, sorry, sorry.

CELIA 2: That's enough sorries. Get ahold of yourself.

(*CELIA starts rocking to the sorries. BERYL 2 pulls BERYL away.*)

Stop that! She won't come back now you idiot!

(*BERYL returns, fascinated by CELIA.*)

CELIA: (*With great effort.*) Oh, I didn't mean nothing. Anything. I'm unusually volatile today. Restive. Opposite of restful, often incorrectly used. The new medication . . .

CELIA 2: That you're not taking . . .

(*BERYL 2 reluctantly comes back.*)

BERYL 2: "Volatile." Quite a vocabulary.

BERYL: I'll be back. Okay? I have to get it from my car. The package.

(*She hurries off. BERYL 2, quite annoyed, mutters in her ear as they go.*)

BERYL 2: Why? Why? Don't go back. This is not a good neighborhood.

CELIA 2: That was close. Remember to smile.

(*She starts to get under the blanket again, hates the smell, then gives up.*)

Why am I hiding? Only you can see me. But you do smell, honey.

(*The two CELIAs smile.*)

CELIA: It's good to have you.

CELIA 2: We have each other, sweetie. But you got to remember not to talk to me out loud when other folks are around. Okay?

CELIA: Okay.

(*The two CELIAs embrace.*)

Oh, I hear her coming! She's coming back! (*In awe.*) She came back.

(*CELIA 2 stands or sits closely behind CELIA.*)

CELIA 2: Unbelievable. Remember. No talking to me. We need stuff. *We always need stuff.*

(*BERYL has a bottle of water and plastic bag stuffed with a can of sardines, a plastic fork and spoon, a hairbrush, a small applesauce container and some packets. BERYL 2 follows, gesturing her disapproval. CELIA's face lights up as BERYL hands her the plastic bag and water.*)

BERYL 2: Okay, you gave her the stuff. Now get away. Get back to your car. Return to the office.

(*BERYL ignores BERYL 2. CELIA eagerly goes through the plastic bag. BERYL motions, asking if she may join her. CELIA is surprised BERYL is still there. BERYL sits down next to CELIA.*)

BERYL: I hope you like sardines. You don't need a can opener.

CELIA: I have a can opener!

(*CELIA 2 looks concerned.*)

CELIA 2: Don't get mad!

(*CELIA calms down.*)

CELIA: My nutritionist says sardines are an excellent source of protein, although the soy bean oil is not the best kind of oil . . .

BERYL 2: Her nutritionist? Oh come on. She wants you to give her the expensive kind, with olive oil? You don't even buy those for yourself!

BERYL: My nutritionist says exactly the same. I love sardines. Actually, the basic store brand—that's what's in the package—they're delicious. I gave you a fork and a spoon too.

CELIA: Ooh, applesauce! Hence the spoon. My *accoutrements*. Do you have another color of socks?

CELIA 2: Honey, are you crazy. Well, yes.

BERYL 2: What does she think this is—shopping? Grey isn't good enough to sit on the sidewalk?

BERYL: I think I only have this color.

CELIA 2: Let's be practical.

CELIA: It's great. And these—what are these?

BERYL: (*A little shyly.*) They're toilet wipes. So you can clean yourself off.

CELIA: Hmmm. I like the hairbrush. (*She starts to brush her hair with it.*) The Portuguese popularized sardines. They fished them so much, so successfully, how did you even find any sardines for me, and then they came to Massachusetts and Rhode Island . . . I speak perfect Portuguese. Do you speak Portuguese?

BERYL: No. I'm not very good with languages.

CELIA: Oh I am. I speak five languages.

CELIA 2: Stop it! Stop it!

CELIA: I really do. I was an extraordinary student. I was on my way to a doctorate . . .

BERYL 2: Now she's on her way to the looney bin . . .

BERYL: I think I have to go.

BERYL 2: Now you're talking.

(CELIA stops brushing her hair and looks longingly at BERYL.)

BERYL: Would you like me to sit with you for a moment?

BERYL 2: No, no, no! She could be dangerous.

CELIA 2: Don't let her get too close. You never know what they're going to pull on you. They want to reintegrate you. Watch out.

CELIA: Oh, yes, yes, yes! Sit with me.

(BERYL sits near CELIA, ready to spring up if necessary. BERYL 2, angry at this disobedience, walks away.)

CELIA 2: Careful! Easy, girl. You got me. You don't need her kind.

(Beat.)

BERYL: Did you ever get your phone back?

(CELIA and CELIA 2 look at BERYL with suspicion.)

I've . . . seen you before, and one time you were very upset because someone took your phone.

(CELIA seriously considers BERYL before answering.)

CELIA: No, I never got it back. Some people are so awful. Why should somebody take my phone? I had it on my cart. Anybody could see it belonged to somebody. It was with all my things.

BERYL: Yes. That wasn't nice. Everyone has to be so . . . careful.

(CELIA nods in agreement.)

BERYL 2: What I really want to know is what you're doing out here on the streets. How could you let this happen to yourself? Don't you have a family? Isn't there somebody who would help you? And if you speak all these languages, couldn't you have gotten a job at some point?

BERYL: I just hope you're all right.

CELIA 2: No she doesn't. Watch out! She thinks you're strange and you smell bad and your clothes are wrong wrong wrong! Look at her purse! It's so nice.

> (*CELIA starts to look closely at BERYL's purse. BERYL pulls back, clutching her purse, getting closer to BERYL 2.*)

BERYL 2: I told you.

CELIA: Sorry. I like your purse. It's pretty.

BERYL: (*Hesitant.*) Thank you.

BERYL 2: You don't know what to say. You don't want to be insulting, but you have to admit, you were worried.

CELIA 2: They're always going to think you're dangerous . . . unsavory. Unsuitable.

CELIA: (*Sadly, agreeing with CELIA 2.*) Un-everything.

BERYL: What?

CELIA: I was just thinking, if I could only go back, and undo everything . . .

BERYL: But none of us can, can we?

CELIA: No.	BERYL: No.
CELIA 2: No.	BERYL 2: No.

BERYL: I'd like us to be able to say "yes" to something.

CELIA: Yes, yes, yes, yes!

BERYL: Do you know about the St. Joseph Center?

CELIA: No. Where is it?

BERYL: It's in Venice.

CELIA 2: Oh little goody two shoes.

CELIA: Venice is far. Is there a bus?

BERYL: I don't know.

BERYL 2: Little Goody Two Shoes.

CELIA 2: Get real! She doesn't take the bus! This is L.A. Nobody with money takes the bus.

BERYL 2: Don't give her money!

CELIA: Could you give me money to go there?

(*BERYL seems torn. She opens her purse.*)

BERYL 2: If you give her five dollars, and tell her to use it for the bus, she'll tell you "don't tell me how to spend my money!"

CELIA 2: We've been down this road before. Say goodbye before she does. Show her. Say bye!

CELIA: Bye. I don't need your money. Get off the sidewalk! Get off! Get away!

(*BERYL and BERYL 2 hurry away, upset.*)

BERYL: What did I do wrong? Should I have given her bus fare? I don't even know what bus fare in L.A. is.

END OF PLAY

THE SCOTTISH LOO

by J. Thalia Cunningham

The Scottish Loo was produced September 20–29, 2019, at the Pittsburgh New Works Festival, Pittsburgh, Pennsylvania. Produced by Prime Stage Theatre. Producing Artistic Director: Wayne Brinda (wbrinda@primestage.com).

Director: Linda Halston

Cast:
LADY MACBETH: Kaitlin Cliber
HILLARY CLINTON: Stephanie Akers

CHARACTERS

LADY MACBETH, 400 years old, but doesn't look it. Ruthlessly ambitious and power hungry. Neither compassionate nor feminine. Otherwise occupied when they handed out maternal genes. Enjoys being a mommy and grandma for material reasons. Thinks *she* wears the breeches in the family. Thinks *she* wears the pantsuits in the family. Suffers from obsessive-compulsive disorder. Meyers-Briggs Personality Type likely but hasn't seen a shrink about it yet.

HILLARY CLINTON, 60s, and looks it. Compassionate in a politically correct way. INTJ (Introversion, Intuition, Thinking, Judgment), but nobody knows for sure.

SETTING

Ladies' restroom at a mythical political convention.

TIME

At a mythological time. Clearly, times, dates, and reality have been pulverized in a Cuisinart. But that's fine, since some things are timeless.

NOTE

Specific race and ethnicity of the actors are unimportant. They could be black, brown, yellow, white, blue, magenta, etc. Lady Macbeth may speak with a vaguely Scottish brogue. Or not.

• • •

Ladies' restroom. Small table, a chair, mirror, box of Kleenex, wastebasket on floor. An indication that toilets are within. A door leads outside to the convention. We hear crowd roaring. LADY MACBETH enters through door in voluminous dress and straw boater with band of red, white, and blue. She makes sure door is shut, walks away, then returns to recheck it. Peers in mirror, scratches at spot on dress. We hear toilet flushing. From folds of dress, LADY MACBETH removes Tide to Go, dots it on the spot, rubs furiously. We hear toilet flushing a second time. HILLARY CLINTON emerges, wearing pantsuit, straw boater with rainbow band, carrying small clutch purse and capacious tote bag. Plops both on table, rummages in handbag, removes Purell sanitizer, which she uses to wash hands.

HILLARY CLINTON: Jesus H. Christ. All that hand shaking.

LADY MACBETH: God knows where their hands have been.

HILLARY CLINTON: I'm worried I'll catch something.

LADY MACBETH: Me too.

HILLARY CLINTON: Are they carrying communicable diseases? Masturbating without washing afterwards?

LADY MACBETH: I know, right? Mind if I borrow your hand sanitizer?

> *(CLINTON passes it. LADY MACBETH uses Purell to wash hands then returns it.)*

HILLARY CLINTON: Keep it. I've got oodles. I go through Purell faster than an intern at a cigar store.

LADY MACBETH: Don't you mean Indian at a cigar store?

HILLARY CLINTON: No, *intern*. And you should say Native Americans. Actually, I believe they went and changed it again. You're supposed to call them Indigenous Peoples. At least this week.

LADY MACBETH: Who? Interns?

HILLARY CLINTON: Indians, which means we just had Indigenous People's Summer. Now that our hands are clean . . . I'm Hillary Clinton.

LADY MACBETH: (*Shaking CLINTON's outstretched hand.*) Lady Macbeth.

HILLARY CLINTON: Wait, are you the same Lady Macbeth from eleventh grade English? I got an A.

LADY MACBETH: The same.

HLLARY CLINTON: You're still here? Or are you a ghost? One of the Living Dead, perhaps?

LADY MACBETH: No, you're getting me confused with Hamlet, Elvis, and low-budget horror films.

HILLARY CLINTON: What in hell have you been doing these past four hundred years?

LADY MACBETH: Busy busy. Productions, films, Spark Notes. Trying to keep up with all this technology.

HILLARY CLINTON: I thought you'd committed suicide.

LADY MACBETH: A lady always has the prerogative to change her mind.

   (*Pulls out flask from folds of dress, checks door, passes flask to CLINTON.*)

This keeps me under partial anaesthesia during this political bullshit. Want a slug?

HILLARY CLINTON: God, yes. Anyone else around?

LADY MACBETH: Coast is clear. They're all out there being earnest and patriotic.

HILLARY CLINTON: (*Gulping from flask.*) Thanks. I needed that. Press thinks I have chronic dehydration. They think I don't drink enough water.

My staff told them, "*You* try telling her what to do." Disgusting public restrooms, and, you know, you drink more, you pee more. What if I fart?

LADY MACBETH: Booze won't help your dehydration.

> (*They pass flask back and forth. LADY MACBETH checks dress in mirror.*)

Maybe you've got chronic dehydration, but I might as well have chronic constipation, since I'm stuck in here until I get out this damned spot.

HILLARY CLINTON: This is not going to be one of those plays where a character quotes Shakespeare every few lines, *is* it?

LADY MACBETH: I guess it depends on what your definition of "is" is.

HILLARY CLINTON: It's a deplorable trend. What happened to your dress?

LADY MACBETH: Idiot mother demanded a photo of me holding her kid. Brat spit up breast milk on my dress.

HILLARY CLINTON: Not exactly the milk of human kindness, eh?

LADY MACBETH: I thought you didn't like plays that quoted Shakespeare. My dress is silk.

HILLARY CLINTON: You should stick to polyester.

LADY MACBETH: I'm sweating like a pig, dearie. If I wore polyester in that crowd, I *would* stick to it.

HILLARY CLINTON: I'm impressed you carry Tide to Go and know what polyester is.

LADY MACBETH: It's important to be au courant.

HILLARY CLINTON: Are you enjoying the convention?

LADY MACBETH: About as much as I enjoy the barber pulling out a rotten tooth with rusty pliers, but at least my barber doesn't hold me hostage for hours while boring me with speeches.

HILLARY CLINTON: Who are you here to support?

LADY MACBETH: My husband. I'm trying to push his sorry ass up the political ladder.

HILLARY CLINTON: Me too. How do your husband's chances look?

LADY MACBETH: Latest polls say not good. It's not enough I run the household and scold lazy servants who refuse to wash the whites separately? No, I have to mastermind his political career as well.

HILLARY CLINTON: Me too. And how does my husband thank me? By screwing around. Yours cheat on you?

LADY MACBETH: Ha! That pantywaist? He doesn't have the balls. He even pads his codpiece. But don't tell.

HILLARY CLINTON: I didn't ask. (*Pause.*) I stood by my man when he said, "I smelled her perfume, but didn't inhale." I'm thinking, why should I support his candidacy? Why not me?

LADY MACBETH: Me too. Maybe we don't have balls . . . but we've got . . . labias of steel.

HILLARY CLINTON: Labias of steel. That's good . . . I always figured I'd use my husband as a stepping stone.

LADY MACBETH: Which will you do first? Stone him or step on him?

HILLARY CLINTON: Neither. It's an overused metaphor.

LADY MACBETH: Wouldn't eliminating them be easier than this inane campaigning?

HILLARY CLINTON: You mean . . . ?

LADY MACBETH: Yup—just kill the competition. Let's murder our husbands and run in their stead.

HILLARY CLNTON: Have patience. I think it might be a virtue. Their power will fuel ours. Eventually.

LADY MACBETH: Don't say "fuel." With environment and climate change issues, it could work against you.

HILLARY CLINTON: But fuel's a more interesting and active verb than "help." I know. How about "galvanize"?

LADY MACBETH: It will make folks think of zinc.

HILLARY CLINTON: So what? Zinc is necessary for a healthy immune system.

LADY MACBETH: Voters won't think of that. They'll think environmental hazards for freshwater organisms.

HILLARY CLINTON: You really meant what you said about trying to be au courant.

LADY MACBETH: My alchemist puts *Reader's Digest* in his waiting room. Screw your virtuous patience. I don't want to hold another drooling baby while smiling demurely for the cameras. (*Reaching into folds of dress, withdraws large butcher knife.*)

HILLARY CLINTON: How'd you get that past security?

LADY MACBETH: This is politics. I network and make connections. Like everybody else.

HILLARY CLINTON: Why in the name of Jeffrey Dahmer did you bring that knife to the convention?

LADY MACBETH: It's political Woodstock out there. I could dive into that swarm of humanity, stab my bastard of a husband, and dissolve into the crowd before anyone discovered who did it.

HILLARY CLINTON: I think you're crazy, but I do admire your verbs. Then what?

LADY MACBETH: Get rid of the knife. Then I'd run for election instead of that codpiece-padded wuss.

HILLARY CLINTON: Don't do it. Our forensics are more sophisticated than whatever you had in Elizabethan times. Did you have forensics back then? They'd figure it out and lock you up.

LADY MACBETH: Loch me up? Where? Like Loch Ness?

HILLARY CLINTON: L.O.C.K. Lock with a "k." Not that lake where the monster lives.

LADY MACBETH: The Loch Ness Monster fable is a load of crap.

HILLARY CLINTON: I'm so relieved you said it's a load of crap. I was afraid you'd say it was fake news.

LADY MACBETH: So what? By then, I'd be the Grand Poobah. Yertle the Turtle, ruler of all I could see.

HILLARY CLINTON: It's too dangerous. Bide your time.

LADY MACBETH: How much more time must I bide? I've been Jonesing for power four hundred years now.

HILLARY CLINTON: You look great. I've been noodling in politics since the mid-1970s and look as old as I feel.

LADY MACBETH: A seventeenth-century skin care line with white lead and honey. Might help your crow's feet.

HILLARY CLINTON: I'm more interested in power than crow's feet. Why don't we join forces? Help each other.

LADY MACBETH: What do you mean?

HILLARY CLINTON: Run for election ourselves. Show voters who's the best man . . . woman . . . for the job.

LADY MACBETH: You mean winning through character assassination instead of the other kind? I don't know . . . I kinda prefer the sort of assassination where my victim doesn't have a blood pressure when I'm done.

HILLARY CLINTON: You kill your husband, your political career would come to a standstill when you're tried for murder and thrown in the slammer.

LADY MACBETH: I'd pardon myself. Anyhow, prison worked out pretty good for Nelson Mandela. And Nehru.

HILLARY CLINTON: Worked out *well*. We'd be a formidable team, you and I, slicing up the opposition into baloney sandwiches. Please, give me the knife.

LADY MACBETH: (*Reluctantly hands over butcher knife.*) Slicing up baloney sandwiches? I'm sick of fixing his lunches. But since you said please, I suppose I could take a stab at it.

HILLARY CLINTON: If we're going to work together, you need to realize that bad puns are deplorable.

LADY MACBETH: If I put the kibosh on bad puns, will you stop using that irritating word?

HILLARY CLINTON: What word? Deplorable?

LADY MACBETH: You just said it again.

HILLARY CLINTON: (*Wipes knife with Kleenex, places it on table, throws Kleenex into wastebasket.*) See? I wiped off your fingerprints, so you won't get into trouble.

LADY MACBETH: What did you mean . . . team?

HILLARY CLINTON: I told you. I'll be the Top Banana, and you'll be the Vice Banana.

LADY MACBETH: No, I'll be Big Kahuna and *you'll* be Vice Kahuna. Or Medium Kahuna, if you prefer.

HILLARY CLINTON: You've got to understand, honey, I've got more experience.

LADY MACBETH: Sez who?

HILLARY CLINTON: If you don't believe me, check my Wikipedia page.

LADY MACBETH: Right. I should believe someone with political aspirations? I'm the one who's strong, fearless. Not afraid of committing murder to get what I want.

HILLARY CLINTON: That's not strong and fearless. It's dumb.

LADY MACBETH: Whitewater wasn't dumb?

HILLARY CLINTON: You know how the media screws stuff up.

LADY MACBETH: What makes you think you're more experienced? I've been around for centuries.

HILLARY CLINTON: Times have changed.

LADY MACBETH: How do you know?

HILLARY CLINTON: I took a lot of history courses at Wellesley.

LADY MACBETH: I do agree with you that women should support each other, but . . .

HILLARY CLINTON: . . . Good. Let's agree I'll be the Big Cheese, and you'll be Vice Cheese. My Baby Gouda.

LADY MACBETH: No. I'll be Numero Uno and you'll be Numero Dos.

HILLARY CLINTON: (*Escalating a bit.*) After I've served my two terms, you'll have my full endorsement.

LADY MACBETH: (*Also escalating.*) Endorsement? You talking about getting me elected or putting my mug on a box of cereal?

HILLARY CLINTON: People know who I am.

LADY MACBETH: You think they don't know who I am?

HILLARY CLINTON: Voters try to forget high school traumas—acne, sex, reading Shakespeare in English class.

LADY MACBETH: You didn't.

HILLARY CLINTON: But I got an A. We'd have a better chance if I'm running as the Big Shot, okay?

LADY MACBETH: *Not* okay. I'll run as . . .

HILLARY CLINTON: (*Lava bubbling in a volcano.*) This has enormous potential. Don't screw it up.

LADY MACBETH: (*Ditto bubbling lava.*) Me? You're the one who's . . .

HILLARY CLINTON: What makes you think you . . . ?

LADY MACBETH: Shut your trap, lavvy heid.

HILLARY CLINTON: *What* did you call me?

LADY MACBETH: Scottish. Means toilet-head. Whatcha going to do about it, lavvy heid? Lavvy heid lavvy heid lavvy heid lavvy heid . . .

> (*HILLARY CLINTON grabs knife with her bare hand, pointing it at LADY MACBETH. Her anger is such that she completely forgets she wiped off LADY MACBETH's fingerprints.*)

HILLARY CLINTON: Why, you . . . you . . . bitchy little . . . I ought to . . .

LADY MACBETH: What? Kill me? If this were one of those plays that quoted Shakespeare, boy, just think of all the options I could use right now.

HILLARY CLINTON: (*Putting knife back on table.*) This is ridiculous. Go ahead. Run on your own platform. You'll realize you passed up an extraordinary opportunity, but . . . fine.

LADY MACBETH: Fine. I will.

HILLARY CLINTON: Fine. We'll go our separate ways, and may the best woman win.

LADY MACBETH: Fine.

> *(They shake hands. Stare at each other. Beat.)*

HILLARY CLINTON: (*Suspicious de-escalation.*) Look, I shouldn't have forced my own ideas of achieving success on you. If you feel you can realize your ambitions more efficiently by murdering your husband, I have no right to tell you what to do or stand in your way. Please accept my apology.

LADY MACBETH: Apology accepted. I admire your moxie, your determination. If only more women had it.

HILLARY CLINTON: We've got to set the example for future generations. We'll show women they can make their dreams come true by following paths of individuality. (*Pause.*) Dammit, I shouldn't have had so much booze. I've got to pee again. Maybe even a Number Two. Even if it's not a Number Two, I'm going to hide in the toilet for a bit. I can't go back out there yet.

LADY MACBETH: I know. It's murder out there. I'm so glad we met. You're one helluva woman.

HILLARY CLINTON: You too. Do I put a hashtag there? (*She moves to exit.*)

LADY MACBETH: (*Motioning towards tote bag.*) Wait, you forgot this.

HILLARY CLINTON: The swag bags were particularly tacky this year, don't you think? At the Russian embassy event, they handed out swag bags with primo vodka and Beluga. But these are deplorable. Any moron who steals mine will likely die of boredom.

> *(She exits towards unseen toilet stalls. Sound of urinating. Listening, to make sure HILLARY CLINTON is occupied, LADY MACBETH takes Kleenex, wraps wads of it carefully around knife so that she avoids getting her fingerprints on it. She exits briefly. We hear HILLARY CLINTON singing from behind stall:)*

. . . OUT CAME THE SUN AND DRIED UP ALL THE RAIN
AND THE ITSY-BITSY SPIDER CLIMBED UP THE SPOUT AGAIN

(We hear scream coming from outside where the convention is taking place. LADY MACBETH re-enters the ladies' room brandishing the knife, bloodied, still wrapped in Kleenex. She listens towards toilet stall. HILLARY CLINTON is still singing. LADY MACBETH uses additional Kleenex to open HILLARY CLINTON's tote bag. She shoves in the knife, which still has HILLARY CLINTON's fingerprints on it, then removes Kleenex, which she stuffs in her dress. She dabs at a minuscule blood spatter, walks towards door, smiling a self-satisfied smile, and sings as she exits:)

LADY MACBETH: . . . THEY ALL RAN AFTER THE FARMER'S WIFE
WHO CUT OFF THEIR TAILS WITH A CARVING KNIFE
DID YOU EVER SEE SUCH A SIGHT IN YOUR LIFE
AS THREE BLIND MICE?
THREE BLIND MICE

(Blackout.)

END OF PLAY

SLIPPED
A Short Play
by Meghan Gambling

Original production by Theatre West as part of WestFest
October 2019

Cast:
WANDA: Saratoga Ballantine
CAROL: Tammy Taylor
MAN: Jason Carmody

Written and directed by Meghan Gambling

CHARACTERS

WANDA TALBERT, 53, attractive, flighty.
CAROL COLLIER, 56, no-nonsense, pragmatic.
MAN, 38, handsome.

SETTING

A budget hotel room in suburban North Carolina.

TIME

Night.

• • •

CAROL and WANDA, sisters, lead a MAN, slumped between them, into a hotel room and arrange him on the bed. He is clearly drunk or drugged or a narcoleptic, maybe all three. WANDA is dressed up, skirt, stockings, full makeup. CAROL wears jeans and looks like she just rolled out of bed, because she did.

(*A moment as they catch their breath.*)

CAROL: What do you want to do?

WANDA: I was hoping you'd have some ideas.

CAROL: I have no ideas whatsoever.

WANDA: Wait for him to wake up, I guess.

CAROL: (*Gesturing towards the man.*) What was your plan for tonight? Was this the plan?

WANDA: No, we were just going to . . . chill.

CAROL: Chill?

WANDA: Yeah, you know, hang out.

CAROL: I understand what the word means, but this is about as far from chill as you can get.

WANDA: How's Dan? Are you guys still . . . ?

CAROL: Still what?

WANDA: What is wrong? Can you just relax?

CAROL: There is a man passed out here and you're asking about Dan.

WANDA: Well I think it's just really impressive that you all keep up such a rigorous schedule. Three times a week for twenty years, that's impressive.

CAROL: What happened, Wanda?

WANDA: I told you already. He's fine, he'll wake up, I didn't realize it would be that strong. I thought he would just be more open . . . to me.

CAROL: Open?

WANDA: Do you think this is what those women were like? The ones Bill Cosby drugged? This out of it?

CAROL: I don't know and I don't want to know.

WANDA: Oh, come on, like you weren't thinking the exact same thing.

CAROL: I can assure you, I wasn't. I'm trying to figure out what to do here, if we should take him to the hospital.

WANDA: No, if he wakes up at the hospital he'll never go out with me again.

CAROL: Wanda. He's never going to go out with you now.

WANDA: Look at him. So handsome. You know twenty years ago I'd be fending someone like him off with a stick. You remember. Men couldn't get enough of me.

CAROL: I'm calling Dan.

WANDA: No, don't do that!

CAROL: He's going to want to know what's wrong. You drag me out of bed at—

WANDA: It's only ten.

CAROL: That's late for me.

WANDA: Look I needed you to help carry him and now he's here so, if you want to go, just go.

CAROL: That's not all you needed me for.

WANDA: Oh, of course. You paid for this, this luxury suite, never let me forget.

CAROL: Well you seemed to forget so I was just reminding you.

WANDA: When have you ever loaned me money and I've forgotten? Why are we even keeping score?

CAROL: How could we keep score? You'd have lost when you were ten years old!

WANDA: That's keeping score.

CAROL: So, what did you give this guy? How did you even get a hold of whatever type of drug this is?

WANDA: I don't know, they were these pills Vince used to take for his hip and he'd like, pass out cold for hours, especially when he took them with vodka. Which, come to think of it, was the only way he took them.

CAROL: But you don't know what they are?

WANDA: No, the label was scratched off. I'm not sure he meant to leave them, but I was chasing him with a shovel so . . .

CAROL: You weren't.

WANDA: It was a plastic one. Not as dramatic. She was waiting in the car so it was all the more pathetic.

CAROL: I'm sorry Wanda.

WANDA: Vince is a piece of shit. I'm better off . . . (*Wanda glances at the man.*)

WANDA: You should have seen his face when he saw me. I walked through the shadows and it lit up, and I got in the light and it just . . . disintegrated.

CAROL: I doubt that's true.

WANDA: I shouldn't have told him I was thirty-nine.

CAROL: What!

WANDA: You try dating in your fifties. It's fucking awful. And the men my age, they all date younger. Should I touch his wiener?

CAROL: Wanda! No.

WANDA: It's probably really small right now. What is that word, phallic?

CAROL: Flaccid.

WANDA: Can I at least touch his biceps? He's like a work of art. All his profile pictures were those body pics like in those Calvin Klein ads.

CAROL: Marky Mark.

WANDA: I can see his six-pack through his shirt, come look at this.

CAROL: (*Getting closer.*) You are totally objectifying him—wow.

> (*Both women marvel at the man.*)

WANDA: I don't think I've ever had this much control over another person. Look how peaceful he is, come on.

(*CAROL surveys him, taking in his vulnerability. Suddenly, a phone starts ringing, jarring them both. WANDA and CAROL quickly realize it's coming from him. The man stirs and they shrink back but he doesn't wake up. Finally, the ringing stops.*)

CAROL: How did he take it? Did you tell him it was something else?

WANDA: No, I just slipped it in his drink, like they do in all those Dateline specials.

CAROL: They don't do it in the specials. They're covering specific cases, it's a re-enactment, not a "how to." Are you telling me it was ground up?

(*The ding of a text. The women notice but keep talking.*)

WANDA: Yes, I had it in a baggie. And I just gave him a little! It wasn't supposed to have this effect I just wanted him to relax!

CAROL: You could go to jail for this. You intentionally gave him drugs to alter his state of mind.

WANDA: Do you think he can hear us? Is it one of those things where he can hear us but he can't move?

(*The phone dings again.*)

CAROL: I don't know, because you don't know what you gave him! When did you do it, while he was in the bathroom?

WANDA: Yes. I chose Randy's bar cause, you know, it's close and near the hotel in case he wanted to come here after. Which wasn't out of the realm of possibility. I mean, Carol, we talked online for like hours, for days, the connection was real. He's from Raleigh, right near where Mom grew up, and he went to Duke, like a really educated guy with a good sense of humor and I was like wow, this guy gets me. I was so nervous going to the bar cause all my pics online are from that Cancun trip from after Marty graduated high school. I don't think I look that different but I guess I do. He was sitting at a table under this huge fluorescent light, I mean the whole place is dark and he chooses this one spot like, waiting to scrutinize me and I saw it—the look pass right over his face, "Nope. No. This isn't what you thought it was. You,

Wanda, are not good enough for me." So fast he excused himself to go to the bathroom, and I started to panic you know—like everything leading up to our meeting was just gone, and there I was alone and I just wanted to say, "It's me, you know, I'm still the same sassy sultry thing I've always been!" I'm sorry I'm not twenty-five, but do I deserve to just be overlooked? Not seen? So yeah, I just put a little in his drink and then, we kept talking and he started to loosen up and I was like, OK, perfect, I can tell him, I can say, "Listen, I put a little something in your drink so we can stop the small talk and really get to know one another." You know he could see me. And I felt guilty but also, I was going to tell him. But he went from zero to sixty so fast and all of a sudden, he's just slumped over on the table, and I'm like, oh my god, and the waiter came by and gave us a weird look, but I just patted him and said, he's had a long day. Just like I would if he was my actual boyfriend.

CAROL: Wanda. You are literally delusional. He's going to wake up, he's going to be pissed and he's going to press charges.

(*The phone rings again. This time the MAN lurches up pulling it out of his back pocket, halfway sitting up.*)

MAN: (*Groggily.*) Hello . . . Hgesihgs hgsieh . . . (*He trails off dropping the phone on the bed.*)

WANDA: (*Hissing.*) I swear it wasn't intentional. You know this about me. Shit. What should we do?

(*CAROL reaches over clicking the phone off.*)

CAROL: Oh, now it's "we"? Five minutes ago, you wanted me to leave.

WANDA: No! Shit. Shit Carol. Shit. I'm sorry I said that. I just feel like you hold everything over my head you know? Every time I need your help—

(*Text ding!*)

CAROL: Well you drag me into these situations—(*Reading the phone.*) Oh shit.

WANDA: What. What?

CAROL: (*Reading the text on his phone.*) "'Find my Friends' says you're at a hotel off Route 70. You were supposed to be here an hour ago, I'm worried man."

WANDA: An hour ago, that means he thought our date would be short! Who is that?

CAROL: It also means that *Phil* is tracking his location.

WANDA: That's impossible.

CAROL: It is entirely possible. Find My Friends is an app you put on your phone so you can always see where someone is.

WANDA: OK that's just creepy. No one would allow themselves to be tracked.

CAROL: It's a safety precaution. Dan and I have it, just I don't know in case we get stuck somewhere with the kids and also, you do know that we're all being tracked all the time—

WANDA: OK don't start with the UFO stuff—

CAROL: No, I'm talking about our data. Do you not read the news? Facebook breaches? Literally how are we related—

(*The phone dings again.*)

WANDA: What? Carol, what.

CAROL: (*Reading the text.*) "Ok I talked to Watkins. Him and Buck and me are coming to where you are. Not trying to cock-block but you've never bailed on babysitting before, so we're coming for you, sorry not sorry bro—"

WANDA: He was supposed to babysit after our date? God this just gets worse and worse.

CAROL: That's what you think is bad? A large group of men are coming here now.

WANDA: Well text him back—

CAROL: I can't, it, it re-locked I don't have his password I can just see the text pop up.

WANDA: OK. The gravity of the situation is suddenly becoming clear to me. I'm sorry, that I'm not more together or something. I still feel bad about all those times I had to stay with you during the divorce.

CAROL: No, don't. The divorce isn't your fault.

(*The phone dings again. WANDA grabs it.*)

WANDA: They're really fucking coming! I gotta get out of here. And we gotta take his phone. Do you think they have cameras in here? Oh, shit!

CAROL: (*Thinking, calm.*) You said "a little" right?

WANDA: A little? A little what?

CAROL: Of the stuff. Of the pill.

WANDA: Yes. Pills. It was actually more than one.

CAROL: Christ. Wanda. This was fully premeditated.

WANDA: (*Defeated.*) I. No. It wasn't supposed to be.

CAROL: OK, so there's still some left?

WANDA: Left?

CAROL: Of the pill. There is still some left?

WANDA: Yes.

CAROL: Take it.

WANDA: What.

CAROL: Take it yourself.

WANDA: Oh my god, why?

CAROL: Then it's like you both got drugged. You can blame it on someone else, you'll wake up next to each other and neither of you know how you got there. I'll chuck his phone, here, give me your purse too, we can pretend it got stolen—

WANDA: Wait, that seems a little too far.

CAROL: Too far? You drugged a man and his *bros* Watkins and Buck are coming for him, I don't think anything is *too far* at this juncture. Here, give me your purse!

WANDA: (*Realizing.*) This is why I call you, Carol. I'm the dumb one, you're the smart one. I'm the hot one you're the—how much do I take?

CAROL: Just a tiny bit, so it's in your system, but you're not actually you know, totally messed up. Ideally it would have the effect on you that you claim to have wanted it to have on him. Just give me whatever is left over and I'll dispose of it.

WANDA: This is perfect. Then it's like we're in this together, we got drugged, we got robbed—it's this big mystery and we have to like, keep going out together in order to crack the case!

CAROL: OK yes, but also, this way you're not charged with conspiracy to commit rape.

WANDA: (*Quietly.*) He's going to see me. He's going to see that I'm old.

CAROL: Wanda. Shut up. You are a beautiful woman. Aren't you relieved you don't have to think about looks all the time? Being in my thirties and forties was exhausting. Slowly watching everything go, now it's gone! Who cares! I'm happier now than I've ever been.

WANDA: You're such an inspiration. Should I snort it?

CAROL: No.

WANDA: I'm kidding.

CAROL: Are you?

(*WANDA pours a little of her concoction into a water bottle from her purse.*)

WANDA: OK. Here goes. You are the best. Like, the best friend and sister I could ever hope for. I love you Carol. Anything you need, anything. I'm here for you always.

(*WANDA takes the water and the drugs in one big gulp as her sister watches approvingly. She lies down next to the MAN, as CAROL grabs his phone and runs out.*)

END OF PLAY

SPEED DATING

by Nedra Pezold Roberts

Original production
Premiere presented by the Center for Performing Arts Bonita Springs,
"Funny Shorts LIVE!" festival, Bonita Springs, Florida, June 14–15, 2019.

Cast:
IRIS: Jennifer Valienta
ART: Aires De Avila, Jr.
Director: Frank Blocker

CHARACTERS

ART, a handsome Artificial Intelligence robot, slightly awkward in this
setting. For the most part, his speech is precise and carefully chosen. He
is sweet, completely guileless.
IRIS, attractive, curious, and approachable. She is unaware that ART is a
robot.
VOICE, the cheerful Event Coordinator, heard but not seen.

SETTING

A speed-dating event. The present.

• • •

*At rise, an empty stage, save for a small table with two chairs. Clearly visible on
the table is a card with a number. The VOICE begins its spiel while the stage is
empty.*

VOICE: Welcome, Speed Daters! Tonight's exciting event offers you the chance to meet face-to-face with interesting people just like you.

> *(IRIS enters, holding a card, and moves around casually, as if looking for her table amidst all the others.)*

Whether you're looking for that someone special or just looking to have fun meeting new people, you've come to the right place! Now, you've all been checked in and given your date cards, so let's get started.

> *(As the speaker continues, IRIS finds her table and sits.)*

Ladies, please take a seat at your designated table and remain there throughout the evening.

> *(A moment later, ART enters, holding his card as if he doesn't quite know what to do with it. Unsure, feeling awkward, he hangs back as his eyes search for the table with his first "date.")*

Men, you will begin your first date at the table corresponding to the number at the top of your card. When the bell is sounded, you will move to the next table on your list. Each date will last seven minutes, with a three-minute pause afterward for each of you to make notes on your Speeding Ticket. All right now, Daters. Ready? Set? Explore!

> *(The bell sounds, and ART moves to IRIS' table.)*

ART: (*Gesturing.*) Hello. May I?

IRIS: Yes, of course.

> *(He sits and extends his hand.)*

ART: I'm Art.

IRIS: Iris.

ART: That's pretty. It's a flower, isn't it? Tall and graceful.

IRIS: (*Smiling.*) Smooth. You get points for that right out of the gate.

ART: Pardon?

IRIS: I like your style, Art. Where are you from?

ART: Pipedream Solutions.

IRIS: No, I mean where were you born?

ART: (*Considering the question.*) Born. That would be here in Silicon Valley.

IRIS: (*Delighted.*) Me, too. I guess that makes us practically neighbors. Tell me, Art, how many of these events have you been to?

ART: This is my first.

IRIS: Ah, a speed dating virgin, huh?

ART: I lack this experience, yes.

IRIS: So what made you decide to come tonight?

ART: My coach sent me. He thought it would help me develop my social skills.

IRIS: In that case, I'll let you go first. Go ahead, hit me with your best question.

ART: (*Shocked.*) I would never hit you.

IRIS: (*Laughing at what she thinks is a joke.*) Then just toss it to me. Don't be shy.

ART: What is the hardest thing you've ever done?

IRIS: Hmmm. Hardest thing. I guess it would be bungee jumping. No, make that karaoke singing. I almost peed my pants with embarrassment. How about you?

ART: This. Meeting women. Talking to them is hard. But my goal is to sense, comprehend, act, and learn. And the best way for me to succeed is to do the hard thing first. After that, the other things will be easy.

IRIS: Interesting philosophy. Would you call yourself a "glass-half-full" or a "glass-half-empty" person?

ART: That alternative makes no sense. Both glasses contain the same amount of liquid.

IRIS: Ah, but perception matters. Anything can have an opposite when viewed from a different enough perspective. Wouldn't you agree?

ART: Yes, I have learned that perspective can shape perception. What is your perspective on attraction?

IRIS: I'm all for it.

ART: But what is it? How does it work?

IRIS: That's getting a bit deep for this kind of event, isn't it?

ART: Deep?

IRIS: Oh, you know. Heavy, philosophical.

ART: On the contrary. This event is designed for "daters" to identify and test attraction. But how can we succeed at that if we don't know what attraction is and how it works?

IRIS: Hey, I'm just here to have fun.

ART: Iris, pardon me, but I think that statement is dishonest. Speed dating is predicated on the need for reasoning and decision-making in the controlled chaos of an uncertain environment. I'm assuming you've attended several of these events precisely in order to do that.

IRIS: Aren't you being presumptuous?

ART: Not at all, since I'm here to acquire that decision-making skill as well.

IRIS: Well, don't take offense, but you're starting from behind the curve. Maybe you should try a little less arrogance and a lot more enjoyment.

ART: Oh. Pleasure. (*Beat.*) You have nice eyes. The shape is nice, too, but I mean the truth inside them. It's nice.

IRIS: Thank you. (*Pause.*) You're on the right track. Keep going. What is the most important thing you're looking for in a person?

ART: Emotions.

IRIS: Emotions?

ART: Um, yes. I can read faces by focusing on the biometric face indicators that identify emotional responses. For example, the tilt of your eyebrows and the widening of your eyes tell me you want to be angry, but something is keeping you pleasant. What is it?

IRIS: (*Smiling.*) Amusement? Or maybe curiosity.

ART: You have a nice smile. It's kind. You know, there are gender differences in facial expressions. For example, women smile more and longer than men. Men show anger more frequently than women.

IRIS: You don't say.

ART: (*Confused.*) But I just did. Was I not clear?

IRIS: (*Enjoying the sweetness of his guilelessness.*) You were very clear. I'm just wondering where that observation came from. Is it from your job? What do you do, by the way?

ART: I answer questions. I provide advice to human systems testers on how to solve problems.

IRIS: You work with computers?

ART: I'm in the technology sector. Artificial intelligence. Cognitive Robotics, to be specific.

IRIS: Ah, thus the interest in attraction. Have you learned to code that emotion yet?

ART: Recognizing an emotion doesn't ensure understanding it. Experience does that.

IRIS: (*Trying to puzzle something out.*) Do I know you? You seem familiar.

ART: (*Confused.*) Yes, I'm Art. Your seven-minute date.

IRIS: No, I mean I think I know you from some place. Have we met before?

ART: I would remember. I'm good at remembering.

IRIS: (*Softening, leaning in.*) It's just that I'm feeling . . . a connection.

ART: (*Pleased.*) I can identify that response. The familiar can often put us at ease so that we feel comfortable with a person or situation. (*He's also leaning in now.*) See? You're relaxed. The corners of your mouth are tipped up. And the angle between the tip of your nose and the upper curve of your lips reads as pleasure. The lips are the most expressive of the facial features.

IRIS: (*Feeling the pull.*) Really? I would have thought it was the eyes. You have really soulful eyes.

ART: Does that mean you are attracted to me?

IRIS: I might be. Too soon to tell.

ART: When will you know?

IRIS: (*Amused.*) Are you for real?

ART: I don't understand that question. (*He reaches for her hand.*) I'm here. You can see for yourself. So I must be real.

IRIS: (*Amused but charmed by his sincerity.*) Point taken.

ART: Then, *are* you attracted to me?

IRIS: Do you want me to be?

ART: I don't know. What does it feel like?

IRIS: Are you telling me you've never been attracted to a woman? Are you gay? Because if you are, then you've come to the wrong dating event.

ART: No. I mean I've come to the right event. My mentor assured me this was an important learning experience. And . . . I'm doing my best. It's just that I don't understand women.

IRIS: No man does, but didn't your mother give you a clue?

ART: I don't have one.

IRIS: A clue?

ART: A mother.

IRIS: Oh, Art, I'm so sorry. That kind of loss is terribly hard to deal with, no matter how old we are. Vulnerability strikes deep when we realize we've suddenly become an orphan.

ART: I don't understand.

IRIS: Seriously?

ART: I don't understand.

IRIS: Are you bereft of all emotion?

ART: I can identify many emotions. I am here to understand attraction.

IRIS: (*On guard now, suspecting something.*) Wait a minute. What is your name, your full name?

ART: I was told we're not allowed to give that information until after the date.

IRIS: Your initials then. What are your initials?

ART: A. I.

IRIS: Oh. My. God. How could I have missed this?

ART: What?

IRIS: I know you! Oh, my god.

ART: I don't understand.

IRIS: You're not some random guy. You're a robot. An Artificial Intelligence robot.

ART: My name is Art. I read faces. I don't understand what yours is saying.

(*Something is happening with IRIS. Her demeanor is stiffening a bit as her circuits begin misfiring, and her responses are now delivered by rote, revealing that she, too, is an AI robot.*)

IRIS: My face. My face. My face is programmed to interact with humans. This doesn't compute.

ART: Your face. The look confuses me. I see surprise but—more. I cannot identify that emotion.

IRIS: I cannot identify that emotion.

ART: Is it attraction?

IRIS: Is it attraction?

ART: I think it is attraction. We seem to be compatible.

IRIS: We seem to be compatible.

(*The bell sounds, signaling the end of the date.*)

VOICE: Okay, ladies and gentlemen, time to change partners and begin your next date. But first, take three minutes to record your impressions and find out if you want to meet again for a real date.

ART: Would you like to leave now? We can go to the coffee shop next door to talk and explore our attraction.

IRIS: Explore our attraction.

>(*They both rise, but IRIS wobbles, needing a little assistance as they leave. ART puts his arm around her waist.*)

ART: What kind of coffee do you drink? I like cappuccino.

IRIS: I like cappuccino.

ART: We have a lot in common. That must be attraction.

IRIS: Must be attraction.

>(*Lights fade.*)

END OF PLAY

SUMMER BREAK

by Cary Gitter

Summer Break was originally produced as part of Rule of 7x7 at the Tank in New York City on June 28 and 29, 2019.

It was directed by Lily Riopelle and featured Michael Grew as SAM and Turna Mete as AMY.

CHARACTERS

SAM, 20s.
AMY, 20s.

TIME

The start of the summer.

SETTING

A beer garden.

NOTE

A slash / indicates an overlap.

• • •

Lights up on AMY and SAM at a beer garden, with steins of beer. He's wearing a fanny pack. It's the start of the summer.

SAM: See, now this is just nice.

AMY: It is . . .

SAM: I love how you just suggested this! Like Sunday night, start of the summer, nothin' goin' on, why not go out to the beer garden? I just feel like that's the kind of spontaneity that keeps our relationship fresh . . .

AMY: You know.

SAM: What?

AMY: No, I actually—I wanted to talk about our relationship.

SAM: You did?

AMY: Yeah! So . . . I've been thinking . . .

SAM: What have you been thinking?

AMY: I've been thinking that maybe we should take a break.

SAM: A break?

AMY: No, not a—I don't mean separating or anything . . .

SAM: Then what do/you—

AMY: I mean a break. From. Monogamy. For the summer.

   (Beat.)

SAM: Oh.

AMY: Yeah!

SAM: When did . . . when did this idea come to/you . . .

AMY: It's just something I've been thinking about lately? I mean, you know, we've been together a couple years now, and things are so great between us. Like we're obviously heading down the old long-term commitment path. So I just thought, hey, why not take a summer to fuck other people? Just get it out of our systems! Spice things up a little—

SAM: You don't think things are spicy?

AMY: No, I mean . . . we have our routine . . .

SAM: Our routine?

AMY: Yeah, you know, fifteen minutes of foreplay, fifteen minutes of fucking, orgasm, orgasm, separate trips to the bathroom, and then lights out and goodnight.

SAM: See, I feel like that's a . . . a beautiful sequence of events . . .

AMY: But there are other ways of doing things!

SAM: What other ways?!

AMY: That's what I wanna find out!

    (Pause.)

SAM: Okay. Okay. I'm trying to process this. Even though you just like sprung it on me in the beer garden . . .

AMY: I thought this would be a nice place to discuss/it . . .

SAM: Yeah, well, honestly, I'm a little, like, taken aback? And kind of hurt . . .

AMY: Sam. Come on. You honestly have no desire to sleep with other people?

SAM: No! I mean . . . no!

AMY: I see you checking out other women on the street!

SAM: Yeah, okay, maybe I like drink them in with my eyes, but that doesn't mean I wanna . . .

AMY: Wow, that is such a cop-out! You just don't want me to fuck other men!

SAM: OF COURSE I DON'T, AMY. The thought of you fucking other men is like the most agonizing, brutalizing nightmare to me! That's why I hate all your ex-boyfriends even though I've never even met them . . .

AMY: Why, because you wanna possess me? You wanna own me?

SAM: No, I just . . . I want sex to be reserved for us! You and me. Exclusively. Is that too much/to . . .

AMY: Forever?

SAM: Yes, forever and ever and ever and ever!

AMY: . . . Jesus. I had no idea you were so close-minded about this stuff. I mean it's [current year]. The patriarchal model of monogamy is totally up for debate right now. I didn't realize you were so like . . . antiquated . . .

SAM: I'm not antiquated! I'm . . . hip to stuff . . .

AMY: Then why are you reacting this way?

(Pause. SAM tries not to be antiquated.)

SAM: All right. But like . . . how would this even work? I mean we live together . . .

AMY: So?

SAM: So, what, I would just like come home from the office one day and see you fucking some other dude in our living room and be like, "WELL, WOULD YA LOOK AT THAT" . . .

AMY: No! We would set ground rules! And one of those rules could be, um, you know, do not bring any strangers home to fuck.

SAM: . . . Oh . . .

AMY: Yeah! It's all about setting boundaries. Keeping it open and honest and transparent . . .

SAM: So like would we tell each other? If we had sex with someone else?

AMY: See, that's an excellent question!

SAM: . . . Thank you?

AMY: That is like totally something we would have to decide on based on our comfort level . . .

SAM: But we'd always use protection, right? I mean 'cause of like diseases and pregnancy/and

AMY: OF COURSE, SAM. YES, WE'D USE PROTECTION. God, who do you think I am? That is like Rule Number One of Open Relationships.

SAM: What about people we know?

AMY: What?

SAM: Would people we know be off limits? 'Cause I feel like maybe, maybe, I could handle you sleeping with a stranger I never have to meet or see or talk to. But someone we both know, someone I have to then like look in the eye, knowing they had relations with you . . .

AMY: I mean . . . yeah, we can . . . discuss that.

SAM: . . . Wait, is there someone specific we know who you wanna sleep with?

AMY: . . . No . . .

SAM: Is it my brother?

AMY: Your brother?

SAM: Yeah, I don't know, I've never said this out loud before, but I just feel like you and Isaac have this like amazing connection that I always feel on the outside of whenever we all get together, and I could totally see that being a thing, I mean . . .

AMY: SAM. WHAT THE FUCK ARE YOU TALKING ABOUT?

SAM: . . . I . . . I don't know . . .

AMY: You're so paranoid. I mean here I thought I was dating this like progressive millennial man who's like open to new things and different perspectives . . .

SAM: I am!

AMY: . . . but you're like this family-values conservative all of a/sudden . . .

SAM: Wait! Hold on!

AMY: What?

SAM: I have another question.

AMY: . . . Okay, what's your question?

SAM: Let's say . . . let's say we did this . . . just for the summer . . .

AMY: (*Sung like a song.*) Until Monday, September 23rd.

SAM: You know the exact date when summer ends?

AMY: Yeah! Like I said, I've been thinking about it!

SAM: . . . Right. So we try this . . . until September 23rd. But what if . . . what if one of us starts like getting a lot of action . . . and the other person isn't getting any at all?

(*Pause. They consider this very real possibility.*)

AMY: I mean . . . I don't think that would happen.

SAM: Amy, come on!

AMY: What . . .

SAM: You know what! You're like this beautiful, sexy woman . . .

AMY: But I'm with you . . .

SAM: Yeah, because I like won you over with my charm and kindness and incredible decency! But that's not gonna work for me if I'm just trying to like pick people up . . .

AMY: Well, losing the fanny pack might help.

SAM: . . . Wow. Did you seriously just bring up the fanny pack right now?

AMY: Yeah, I brought up the fanny pack.

SAM: You know why I wear the fanny pack, Amy.

AMY: Not really.

SAM: BECAUSE IT'S A CONVENIENT WAY FOR ME TO CARRY THINGS I NEED, LIKE CHAPSTICK, HAND SANITIZER, BAND-AIDS, AND SNACKS. AND I THOUGHT YOU THOUGHT IT WAS ENDEARING.

AMY: I DO THINK IT'S ENDEARING, BUT I'M PRETTY SURE I'M IN THE MINORITY.

SAM: WELL, I'M NOT LOSING THE FANNY PACK.

AMY: FINE, KEEP THE FUCKING FANNY PACK.

(*Beat.*)

SAM: You know what? I don't think I wanna do this summer-break thing.

AMY: Oh, you don't?

SAM: Nope. Nope. I don't think it's a good idea. But hey, thanks for bringing it/up . . .

AMY: Then I think I wanna break up, Sam.

SAM: . . . What?

AMY: Yeah . . .

SAM: Break up? What are you talking about? Why?

AMY: (*A fast-moving torrent.*) Because. Because. Because I love you, Sam. I love you and your fanny pack and your goodness. And these last two years have been—I mean when you took me on that first date to the Hayden Planetarium and you like knew more about astronomy than the tour guide did, I was like, who is this guy? I love this guy. And we have so much fun. You are like the only person I wanna play my weird songs to when I first write them. And living with you is—I mean you're so neat! You're fucking neat! I leave a mess and run out the door and I come home and you've tidied it up! That's—Yeah. I'm happy. I'm happy with you, Sam. But—God—but we're young, aren't we? We're in our twenties. We have potentially like seventy years of life left. And I—yeah—I wanna have sex. With other people. For a little bit. Because they have different bodies. And do different things. And I'm curious, okay? I'm curious. And—and—and lustful. I AM YOUNG, AND I AM LUSTFUL. And okay, maybe you're not into that! Maybe you want just me! That's flattering! That's fine! But for you to just like dismiss it, to get all scared and timid—I don't think I can be with a person who can't even like talk about this stuff or, or, or consider finding a compromise. You know? So yeah, I love you, but if you're just like completely closed off to the possibility of change and growth and exploration, then . . . I don't think this is gonna work.

(*Long pause.*)

SAM: . . . I wanna be open, Amy. I just . . . I like what we have.

AMY: I do too.

SAM: And I don't wanna lose you to some random guy who's like amazing at sex.

AMY: You wouldn't lose me.

SAM: Can I . . . think about it?

AMY: Sure. Of course.

(Sam takes off his fanny pack.)

What are you doing?

SAM: You're right. If I'm gonna get fucked this summer, the fanny pack's gotta go.

AMY: It was a long time coming.

(Grabs the fanny pack, tosses it offstage.)

Come here.

(SAM leans across the table. AMY meets him, and they kiss. Then she raises her stein of beer.)

To . . . a potentially interesting summer.

SAM: . . . Yeah. To that.

(They clink glasses. Look at each other.)

(Blackout.)

END OF PLAY

TELEPHONES AND BAD WEATHER

by Steve Yockey

Originally produced by
City Theatre in Miami, Florida
May 30–June 23, 2019

LAVERN: Hannah Richter
BRENDA: Lindsey Corey
SCOTT: Gregg Weiner
DISCIPLES: Katherine Berger, Therese Callison, Natalia Quintero's-Riestra,
Zye Reid, Emily Rivera
BOOMING VOICE: Steve Shapiro

Director: Andy Quiroga
Artistic Director: Margaret M. Ledford
Set Design: Jodi Delaventura
Lighting Design: Eric Nelson
Sound Design: Steve Shapiro
Costume Design: Ellis Tillman
Property Design: Natalie Taveras

CHARACTERS

LAVERN, a pleasant but very confused neighbor.
BRENDA, a wife, wired, frazzled, barely holding it together.
SCOTT, a husband, relentlessly positive and confident.

DISCIPLES, a group of "true believers" (doomsday cultists) who are way too excited about climate change.

BOOMING VOICE, a mysterious caller with a lot of instructions.

NOTE

This all moves very quickly. It's fast and fun. It's not thoughtful.

When the *BOOMING VOICE* speaks on the rotary telephone, it is terrifyingly loud and broadcast through all speakers in the theater.

The National Weather Service (US) describes moderate flooding as involving some inundation of structures and roads near streams, with some evacuations; major flooding involves extensive inundation of structures and roads and significant evacuations.

> *"If temperatures were 3C warmer on average, Hurricane Katrina, which resulted in nearly 2,000 deaths when levees breached near New Orleans in 2005, would've been worse, with around 25% more rainfall. Cyclone Yasi, which hit Australia in 2011, would have had around a third more rain, while the deluge during Gafilo, a huge storm that killed more than 300 people in Madagascar in 2004, would have been 40% more intense."*
>
> The Guardian
> November 2018

• • •

A suburban living room with a very aggressive thunderstorm raging outside. Everything else is pretty normal except for the small group of DISCIPLES to one side, all in what looks like child's pose. They are fully surrounded by dozens of kitchen glasses and plastic cups. Various sizes, but all full of water. They quietly hum a steady tone. Suddenly there is a violent knocking on the front door. BRENDA enters the living room heading toward the door. She stops, looks at the group of DISCIPLES, and sighs. She shouts at them.

BRENDA: This is a living room! (*She claps twice succinctly to get their attention.*) A living room!

> (*Nothing. She continues over and opens the door. Lighting cracks as LAVERN charges inside. She has a wet raincoat on and she's carrying something bundled up in a towel.*)

LAVERN: Oh thank goodness you answered!

BRENDA: Good grief, Lavern, get in here.

LAVERN: It's really coming down out there. I can't remember the last time we had rain like this. I got soaked through just running over from my house and I didn't . . . who are, Brenda, what's going on in here?

BRENDA: Oh just ignore them. They were outside until it started raining.

LAVERN: It's been raining for two weeks. These people have been in your house since then doing, what are they doing? Is that yoga? Why is there a yoga class in your living room? Honestly, that huge construction project Scott has going on in your backyard is strange enough, now this?

BRENDA: Oh, you think my husband's "construction project" is strange?

LAVERN: Well, I thought it was a very elaborate pergola, but it clearly it isn't.

BRENDA: No, it isn't.

LAVERN: And there's been a lot of talk in the neighborhood about how Scott is starting to "drift" across your property lines with the construction. I've been defending you. I've been telling people it's an avant-garde guesthouse, just so you know.

BRENDA: Thank you, but let's ignore that too, all right?

LAVERN: You have quite a list of things to ignore.

BRENDA: Just the two things. Now why on Earth are you out in this mess?

LAVERN: Because I need you to take this back.

> *(She removes the towel to reveal a sherbet-colored 1980s rotary dial phone. She holds it out for BRENDA to take. It's clear BRENDA's not going to take it. Instead, she quickly looks toward the group of people, all still bowed down, and whispers desperately.)*

BRENDA: You said you would keep it at your house for me.

LAVERN: Well, I didn't have all of the information when I agreed to that.

BRENDA: It's an old phone, what more information do you need?

LAVERN: It keeps ringing. It won't stop ringing at all hours. The sound is disturbing. The frequency of the calls is disturbing. And the fact that it's not plugged into anything is very disturbing. So take it back.

BRENDA: Lavern, I understand how this might be a little unpleasant, but we've been friends for a long time and I have never asked you for anything.

LAVERN: Brenda, we are neighbors. Right now, we're neighbors. If you want to be friends, then take your spooky phone back.

(LAVERN holds it out as if to say, "You see?" Suddenly, the DISCIPLES sit up in unison. Each DISCIPLE grabs one of the glasses littered around them and splashes water in their own face. Then they all look to the sky.)

Answer the call!

DISCIPLES: What is wrong with you people?

LAVERN: Answer the call!

DISCIPLES: No.

(The phone stops ringing. The DISCIPLES all settle back into their bowing positions and begin humming again.)

BRENDA: It's so frustrating, I don't mind telling you. I'm going to have to get that rug steam cleaned when it's all said and done, I just know it.

LAVERN: Brenda, you take this phone from me.

(BRENDA reluctantly takes the phone.)

BRENDA: I'm sorry. All the rain started and I just thought if I got it out of the house then maybe things would calm down a little. But clearly that didn't work. And it wasn't fair of me to try to unload it on you.

LAVERN: What does the rain have to do with it? Who are these people?

BRENDA: It'll sound . . . all right, well, they're disciples. I suppose they are like Biblical disciples.

LAVERN: Disciples?

BRENDA: That's right. Disciples of Scott.

LAVERN: Your Scott? Your husband Scott has disciples?

BRENDA: Yes, Lavern, because apparently he has been chosen by God and it's every bit as crazy as it sounds and I'm doing my very best to hold it together, but I would honestly say that our marriage is in a very complicated place right now, a very difficult, touch-and-go kind of place and the phone really isn't helping so I just thought if I could get a little break from it then I might not go insane. So there you have it.

LAVERN: Have you . . . have you been drinking?

BRENDA: Oh Lavern, I wish. I really do wish I were at least a little tipsy.

LAVERN: Your husband has been chosen by God?

BRENDA: So he tells me. God never speaks to me directly. He kind of calls and shouts things at Scott, ordering him around, telling him to do things.

LAVERN: To do what, exactly?

BRENDA: To build an ark.

LAVERN: Oh come on, you expect me to believe that?

BRENDA: Not even a little bit. But you asked, so I'm being honest. I'm too frazzled and emotionally exhausted to be anything but honest. Global warming is going to result in horrible flooding, among other things, and my husband has to build a boat. How do you like that?

LAVERN: I don't, as it happens. And I don't really believe in global warming.

BRENDA: Out of all this, that's the part you don't believe in? That's remarkable.

LAVERN: I thought I saw on the news "global warming" was going to make things hotter? And we just had the worst winter on record. And if it's getting warmer, isn't it supposed to mean less water?

BRENDA: Ask the people in Miami about that?

LAVERN: I've never been to Miami.

BRENDA: There's a difference between climate and weather, Lavern. Climate change is the Earth gradually getting hotter over a long period time. But the changes to weather in the short term, destructive winters, floods, extreme drought, will be quite catastrophic. I've been reading up on it. Are you sure I can't get you some tea?

(The phone starts ringing.)

Damn it.

(Again the DISCIPLES sit up in unison. Each DISCIPLE grabs one of the glasses littered around them and splashes water in their own face. Then they all look to the sky.)

DISCIPLES: Answer the call!

BRENDA: Can I get you anything? Some tea maybe?

DISCIPLES: Answer the call!

BRENDA: Fine!!

(She answers the phone and immediately holds out the receiver toward the DISCIPLES. A BOOMING VOICE fills the entire space! It speaks with speed and intention, frustration and anger. LAVERN has to cover her ears. It's that loud.)

BOOMING VOICE: I've given you free will! I've given you intellect! I've given you science! I've given you the tools to correct these grievous mistakes of global warming before it's too late! Heed my words before the floods come! They will only be the beginning!

(The call ends. BRENDA hangs up the phone. The DISCIPLES all settle back into the bowing positions and begin humming again.)

LAVERN: That was . . . that was . . . .

BRENDA: We really don't know. It could be God or it could just be an apocalyptic message. Oh, like in the Old Testament when God speaks through some other messenger. Like a burning bush or an angel or something. I've been reading up on that, too. And a lot of legal books. I'm considering divorce.

LAVERN: Oh! Oh no, are you okay?

BRENDA: Not at all. Don't tell Scott. He's very "dedicated" to all of this.

(SCOTT comes in from the back of the house. He's shaking out a wet umbrella. He has on dress shoes, slacks, a dress shirt with the sleeves rolled up, and a pencil behind his ear. He's also carrying a hammer.)

SCOTT: Brenda, did you happen to get to the hardware store? I'm fresh out of screws and I don't think that . . . Oh, Lavern. How are you doing?

LAVERN: Oh, I'm fine, just fine. Fine. Everything's fine. I just, I just needed to bring your phone back.

(SCOTT sees the phone and lights up!)

SCOTT: Where did you find it? We've been so worried. We looked everywhere, didn't we, Brenda? I took a full day away from boat building to search.

LAVERN: So I, uh . . . I took it by mistake. Silly me! I used to have one just like it?

BRENDA: You don't have to do that, Lavern. I gave it to her. And I couldn't go to the hardware store because the streets are flooded and also I didn't want to.

SCOTT: You gave away the phone?

BRENDA: I gave it to her because I needed a break from the ringing, from everything, and you don't want to hear that so here we are.

(The phone starts ringing.)

Perfect.

(Again the DISCIPLES sit up in unison. They splash water in their own faces. Then they look to the sky.)

DISCIPLES: Answer the call!

SCOTT: We need to have an honest talk about this.

DISCIPLES: Answer the call!

(He answers the phone and immediately holds out the receiver toward the DISCIPLES. A BOOMING VOICE fills the entire space! It speaks with speed and intention, frustration and anger. LAVERN covers her ears again.)

BOOMING VOICE: Scott. You must build an ark from cypress wood and coat it with pitch inside and out before the floods! It must be three hundred cubits long, fifty cubits wide, and thirty cubits high for all the animals! This will be too much room for men have already killed many species! But do it anyway!

(The call ends. SCOTT hangs up the phone. The DISCIPLES all settle back into the bowing positions and begin humming again.)

SCOTT: I mean it's pretty clear.

LAVERN: Does it have to be so loud?

BRENDA: Okay, Scott, you want to have an honest talk about this?

LAVERN: Oh, should I be here for this?

BRENDA: You can't build a boat. And you certainly can't build a boat that big alone.

SCOTT: Then help me.

BRENDA: We can't do it by ourselves either.

SCOTT: Not with that attitude. Honey, I never imagined this would happen. I'm no one special, but apparently I can make a difference. And it feels good to know that I can do that. We can do that. And I love you.

BRENDA: I love you too, but that doesn't fix things. You don't know anything about boats. Especially boats that big. I don't know what a cubit is but he wants it to be a lot of cubits. You don't even have boat building clothes, or rainy weather clothes. Just look at you. Why you? Why us?

SCOTT: If not us then who? What if everyone else waits for someone else to do it?

BRENDA: I don't know! But it doesn't have to be us!

SCOTT: Brenda, please don't say that.

BRENDA: I am saying it, I'm saying in front of God and everyone, you, Lavern, your wet disciples!! I didn't sign up for this, okay?

SCOTT: We were chosen.

BRENDA: He doesn't ever talk to me, you were chosen. And you're a dentist, for God's sake. We eat out all the time because neither of us can cook, we can't even make ramen and you're supposed to build an ark?! I honestly don't think I have the strength to do this, Scott. I do not have the strength.

(She collapses onto the couch, distraught. The phone starts ringing. The DISCIPLES sit up in unison. They splash water in their own faces. Then they look to the sky. While this is happening, BRENDA screams at it. LAVERN sits next to her on the couch and comforts her.)

DISCIPLES: Answer the phone!

SCOTT: I have to answer it. I'm sorry.

DISCIPLES: Answer the phone!

(*SCOTT answers the phone, holding it away from his ear like the last few times. But this time there is no BOOMING VOICE. He looks at it quizzically and holds it up to his ear. Then carefully . . .*)

SCOTT: Hello?

(*He holds the receiver out to BRENDA.*)

Honey, it's for you?

(*The DISCIPLES gasp in unison. It's such an honor! LAVERN snaps at them.*)

LAVERN: Oh, be quiet.

(*SCOTT gestures for BRENDA to take it.*)

BRENDA: I don't think I should.

SCOTT: It's up to you.

(*BRENDA tentatively takes the receiver and holds it up to her ear.*)

BRENDA: Hello?

(*Brilliant light shines down on BRENDA and the rest of the lights dim a bit. Everything is quiet except the storm that continues to rage outside. We can't hear what's being said, but someone is talking to her. This sequence takes as long as it needs to . . .*)

No no, I know you're not the one that caused the flooding this time. (*She gasps. Then she covers her mouth in shock. Then she grips the receiver tightly, bad news. Then she begins to cry.*)

It's just such a shame is all. (*Then she smiles with understanding through the tears. Then she smiles more and nods her head "yes" a few times.*) Yes, I suppose we did have lots of chances to fix it. (*Then she nods her head "yes" again a few times. Then she looks over at SCOTT for a moment.*) Yes, he does need rain boots. I told him.

(Then she laughs through her tears of joy. Then she hangs up the phone. Everyone's looking at BRENDA as the lights restore. She's wiping away her tears. LAVERN takes BRENDA's hand. She looks at her and nods.)

LAVERN: What did the voice say?

(BRENDA hesitates, then stands up and clutches the phone to her chest.)

BRENDA: You know what? Noah didn't know how to build boats either and I suppose he did okay. If he could do it, why can't we? Let's build a boat.

END OF PLAY

TWO ARTISTS TRYING TO PAY THEIR BILL

by Lucy Wang

Two Artists Trying to Pay Their Bill first appeared in the Tapas IV: The Great Divide at the Academy Theatre in Hapeville, Georgia, June 7–23, 2019.

The play was directed by Janine Leslie.

Kirstin Popper played WANG, Dharma Moreau played CHEN, and Ryan Cunningham played the RESTAURANT OWNER.

CHARACTERS

WANG, F, emerging playwright, any age, any ethnicity.
CHEN, F, emerging composer, any age, any ethnicity.
RESTAURANT OWNER, M, any age, any ethnicity.

SETTING

A restaurant, anywhere.

TIME

The present.

• • •

Open with some upbeat music. WANG and CHEN are polishing off their meal. The RESTAURANT OWNER approaches table or dining booth with a pitcher of water.

OWNER: So, ladies, did you enjoy your meal?

CHEN: Immensely.

WANG: Simply delicious.

OWNER: Excellent. Would you like more water? It's sparkling, it's organic and it's EPA-approved.

WANG: Oh yes, we must stay hydrated.

OWNER: Always. Can I get you two anything else? Something sweet?

WANG: Chen?

CHEN: It's up to you. I'm good either way.

OWNER: Perhaps some artisan-grown peace, love, and understanding?

WANG: What kind of dessert is that?

OWNER: The kind you inhale slowly. Very slowly. (*Inhales an invisible joint, deep breath in.*) It's so good. So good you have to share.

WANG: Love to, but I have a sore throat. (*Coughs.*)

CHEN: We both have to get back to work. The check, please.

OWNER: Very well. Your loss. Whenever you're ready.

   (*Slams check face down on the table and leaves. WANG grabs check.*)

WANG: Oh my god, this can't be right.

   (*Hands CHEN the check.*)

CHEN: One thousand dollars for two house salads and two Cornish hens. This has to be a mistake.

WANG: A horrible mistake. Grab us a menu.

CHEN (*Grabs menu.*) This is definitely not the same menu. We would have ordered one house salad. To share.

WANG: Are you kidding me? We would have walked out.

CHEN: You're right. How much you got? This menu says the place only takes cash.

WANG: Must be a misprint. Who carries a thousand dollars in cash?

CHEN: Not us!

WANG: Great. This is all I got. (*Sings, lays down a ten-dollar bill.*) Alexander Hamilton. (*Normal.*) You?

CHEN: What a coincidence. I also have (*Sings, also lays down a ten-dollar bill.*) Alexander Hamilton.

OWNER: What's the matter with customers today?! Everyone thinks they have talent.

WANG: I have an idea. You know how Picasso used to pay for his meal with a painting . . .

CHEN: So did Andy Warhol!

WANG: Soup or art?

CHEN: Art.

WANG: We're cool artists, right?

CHEN: The coolest!

WANG: We can impress him with our super fancy resumes. Did you bring yours?

CHEN: I never travel without proper ID.

> (*WANG and CHEN whip out their resumes written on long scrolls. They unfurl long Chinese scrolls or paper towel rolls with their credits.*)

WANG: We can graffiti the wall with Wang and Chen ate here.

CHEN: Sat in this very seat. (*Snaps a selfie.*)

WANG: The worst that can happen is we wash some really dirty dishes. These hands were made for washing . . .

CHEN: Yikes. Not mine. My hands are musical instruments.

(*Summons OWNER with her lovely hands.*)

OWNER: Yes?

CHEN: We'd like to introduce ourselves.

OWNER: How sweet.

CHEN: I'm Chen. Perhaps you've heard of me.

OWNER: Nope.

WANG: Chen is a most famous musician.

CHEN: And Wang, a renowned playwright.

OWNER: Nope. Never heard of either of you. Then again I don't get out much.

WANG: Perhaps you gave us the wrong menu. The menu posted online . . .

OWNER: The menu with the cheap, bargain basement lunch specials.

CHEN: Yes! That menu.

OWNER: Sorry. My bad.

WANG: What a relief. We can pay for our lunch after all.

OWNER: Are you kidding me? I can't afford to give my food away at those prices.

WANG: But that's what you were charging yesterday when we walked by.

OWNER: Ah. That was yesterday. Today, I received my first five-star review. Five stars!

WANG: Congratulations.

CHEN: That's fantastic.

OWNER: So you understand. No more freebies.

CHEN: We want to pay . . .

WANG: . . . What you were charging yesterday.

CHEN: Here's twenty bucks.

OWNER: Twenty bucks?!

CHEN: Twenty-five if you let us use a credit card?

OWNER: For years I gave my food away. For the "free" exposure. Word of mouth.

CHEN: We feel your pain. I can't afford to give my music away for free and yet I have over and over again.

WANG: I hate it when theaters charge money to see my plays and pay me nothing! Oh we'll put your name in the program. You'll get some publicity. Which will generate sales. I wish!

CHEN: Have you ever tried to pay your landlord with a *New York Times* review?

WANG: We have.

OWNER: Did it work?

CHEN: Sadly, no.

OWNER: So you'll pay me.

WANG: Of course.

CHEN: You know how Picasso used to pay for his meals with a painting?

OWNER: You two can paint? Fantastic. This place could definitely use a five-star touchup now that I'm expecting hordes of people demanding a five-star experience. Let me show you around.

CHEN: Oh no. We can't paint.

OWNER: No?

WANG: Actually we were wondering if Chen could pay you with music, and I could pay you with my writing.

OWNER: Are you two nuts? What kind of writing, what kind of music?

WANG: Well, I could write a play about you, for you, for a loved one? I could even write one about someone you hate. Villains make the most interesting characters.

CHEN: Revenge is catchy.

WANG/CHEN: (*Singing from* Chicago.) "He had it coming . . ."

OWNER: A play. Do I look like I have time to go to a play?

WANG: Letter to your "favorite" politician? A letter of protest, a business plan, or perhaps a love letter. Surely, there must be someone you wish to impress.

CHEN: And I could write you a song. Whenever anyone walks in, they could hear your song.

WANG: Your song in every ear.

OWNER: An earworm.

CHEN: Your very own personal earworm.

OWNER: This song would have to have a good beat. I like to dance. It keeps me on my feet which is important in my profession.

CHEN: Of course.

WANG: We could put on a show right here, to celebrate your new five-star review. Five-star revue (perhaps high steps, high kicks) for a five-star review—get it?

OWNER: I am expecting big crowds. Big, big crowds of picky eaters. Gluten-free, vegetarian, keto, paleo, vegan, wheat belly, Whole30. Dear me, what have I done to deserve this?!

CHEN: Perfect. We know how to entertain the masses. We have plenty of experience . . .

WANG: Being women. We were cultivated to please.

OWNER: You can please everybody?

CHEN: We can . . . learn! Everybody Wang . . .

WANG: . . . Chen Tonight!

> (CHEN and WANG dance.)

OWNER: Interesting moves, but you two still owe me a thousand bucks. In cash.

CHEN: Oh dear.

WANG: Don't be so hasty. My first play won an award from the Kennedy Center. My papers are archived at the Huntington Library. Stick with me and we'll make herstory.

CHEN: My music has been performed in Carnegie Hall and Walt Disney Hall. How do you get to Carnegie Hall? Me!

OWNER: One thousand bucks or I call the cops.

CHEN: Aw come on, have a heart, you were a struggling restaurant owner just yesterday.

OWNER: I've evolved.

WANG: Let us pay another way. You're expecting a lot of people any minute now, which means you're going to have a ton of dirty dishes.

CHEN AND WANG: (*Waving their hands.*) These hands were made for washing. Expediting. Bussing.

OWNER: You two are driving me crazy. I sure hope I don't get a lot of customers like you.

CHEN: You never know. Could be worse. A lot worse.

WANG: That's it. What if Chen and I pay you with something guaranteed to drive people like us out of your lives? C'mon, aren't there some people you'd like to see a lot less of?

OWNER: Oh yeah. Now you're talking. People can be pretty disappointing. And then they give you a scathing review on social media.

WANG: Chen's famous for composing "experimental music" that soothes and transports the soul. Outta here.

(*Several phrases of CHEN's music. Experimental, dissonant.*)

OWNER: Aiya! That sounds like a broken tape recorder.

CHEN: And Wang's famous for being edgy and provocative. She's so funny she's scary.

WANG: Did you know in Mandarin, penis is affectionately called Ji-Ji, Chirping Chicken—sounds yummy, doesn't it! But vagina in Mandarin is Yin Dao, the path to death and darkness, and the sewer.

OWNER: That's revolting.

WANG: The Japanese word for balls: Kintama. Worth his weight in gold. Gold! Japanese vagina: Asoko. "There." Put "that" in "there."

OWNER: Awful.

WANG: Our language heavily favors men. Men have seminal moments. Women have yeast infections.

CHEN: I think the next time you accomplish something great, like collaborating with us, you should call it a vaginal moment.

OWNER: But I'm a guy. Guys don't have vaginal moments.

WANG: Why not? Women have been having seminal moments in their careers for centuries.

CHEN: You don't discriminate against women, do you?

OWNER: Hey, some of my best friends identify as female.

WANG: Well then, this is your chance to make your vaginal moment legendary.

CHEN: We'll give you six stars. Shine on!

WANG: Shine on!

OWNER: You two are incorrigible. Feminists.

CHEN: We're your mothers. Sisters. Customers. Friends. We've supported you for years.

OWNER: This hotshot reviewer is female.

CHEN: They say the future is female.

OWNER: Who is they? Money-grabbing politicians who promise lower taxes and universal healthcare?

WANG: Exactly. Whenever unwanted solicitors come banging on your door . . .

CHEN: Demanding money . . .

WANG: Selling magazines or eternal salvation . . .

CHEN: Customers who overstay their welcome . . .

OWNER: Like you two?

CHEN: Much worse. At least we have talent and we work hard.

WANG: Customers who threaten to write you a scathing review unless you give them special treatment . . .

OWNER: I'll give them some peace, love, and understanding unfiltered.

CHEN: Hey, you almost gave that to us.

OWNER: I offered you organic.

WANG: You know they're coming after you, after this five-star review. Expectations have been increased exponentially.

CHEN: Through the stratosphere. Wherever there's hype, there's loud disappointment.

OWNER: This hotshot reviewer ruined my life. Now everybody and their mother wants to eat here.

CHEN: At these prices? I doubt it.

OWNER: You'd be surprised. Rich people are weird.

WANG: So do we have a deal?

OWNER: Let me get this straight. You two write me a song and dance that I can use in perpetuity, and you two get to eat here for free in perpetuity.

WANG: Well, sure . . . as long as your business is open.

CHEN: Which might not be long considering what you charge.

OWNER: Or it could be forever.

CHEN: Nothing lasts forever.

WANG: Then again, it could. Look at us, Chen. We beat the odds.

OWNER: Me too. No one thought my restaurant would last when I opened seven years ago. The odds were against me.

CHEN: Odds are always against you, but odds are not prophecy.

OWNER: So this restaurant could be open ten years from now.

WANG: It could. Because . . . . believe it or not . . .

OWNER: People are strange.

WANG: Very. Just look at us. Two female artists trying to pay our bill creatively.

OWNER: You're asking me to support two female artists I've never met before.

CHEN: Cross the Rubicon. Be creative.

WANG: Please. We support each other.

OWNER: The future is female with many curves.

CHEN: We're gonna be so good together. So good that . . .

OWNER/CHEN/WANG: Everybody Wants to Wang Chen Tonight!!!

(Fade out with OWNER, CHEN, and WANG singing and dancing to a made-up, upbeat song "Everybody Wang Chen Tonight.")

END OF PLAY

WHOA MEANS NO

by Erik C. Hanson

Whoa Means No was produced by Boston University Playwrights as a part of Boston Theater Marathon XXI. It was directed by Mara Dale. Show dates occurred at the Calderwood Pavilion on May 19, 2019.

The cast was as follows:
GUY: Arlen Shane Hancock
GIRL: Anitra Little

CHARACTERS

GUY, 20s, any race, any body type.
GIRL, 20s, any race, any body type.

SETTING

The living room of an apartment.

TIME

Late evening.

• • •

Darkness. Movement on the couch.

GIRL: Whoa!

(Lights come up immediately as a GUY and GIRL separate from their intimate embrace.)

GUY: What's the matter?

GIRL: Whoa-whoa.

GUY: What?

GIRL: I didn't . . .

GUY: You didn't . . . ?

GIRL: . . . consent to that.

GUY: You . . .

GIRL: I did not.

GUY: All right.

GIRL: Not all right.

GUY: I, you . . .

GIRL: Not me. Just you.

GUY: I'm . . . so confused.

GIRL: Out.

GUY: Out?

GIRL: I'd like you to leave please.

GUY: In a minute.

GIRL: Not in a minute.

GUY: You have to explain.

GIRL: I already did.

GUY: You can't . . .

GIRL: Already did.

GUY: Please explain more.

GIRL: I'll call the cops if you don't leave.

GUY: Cops?

GIRL: Don't think I won't.

GUY: I won't think that. Just explain what I did and I'll go.

GIRL: You know what you did.

GUY: A lot's happened since. I need a reminder.

GIRL: You can't be this dense.

GUY: And you can't be this vague.

GIRL: Vague?

GUY: Yes!

GIRL: I'm being v . . .

GUY: Very. Vague.

GIRL: You—I don't want to say it.

GUY: Who but me would hear it?

GIRL: I don't like to say things like that.

GUY: This isn't dirty talk. You're simply recounting what happened.

GIRL: Still.

GUY: (*Standing.*) You know what? I will go.

GIRL: You're going?

GUY: I don't need an explanation.

GIRL: Typical guy. Walk away scot-free, and act like you did absolutely nothing wrong.

(*GUY stops at the door.*)

GUY: I didn't think I did anything wrong!

GIRL: Why would you?

GUY: What was it? Tell me.

GIRL: I . . .

GUY: What didn't you consent to? (*Silence.*) You delaying your response means I'll be here longer. (*Silence.*) Well . . .

GIRL: I didn't say you could grab down there.

GUY: Did I *grab*?

GIRL: It . . .

GUY: I merely put my hand . . .

GIRL: There was nothing "merely" about it.

GUY: I put my hand on your . . .

GIRL: You learn that move from our current president?

GUY: You guided my hand towards that area. *You* did.

    (*GIRL holds her ears.*)

Why are you holding your ears?

GIRL: WHAT?!

    (*GUY motions for her to lower her hands. She does.*)

GUY: Why are you holding your ears?

GIRL: I don't want to hear anymore.

GUY: I'll stop.

GIRL: Were you going to stop earlier?

GUY: I stopped when you said—I forget what.

GIRL: I said whoa.

GUY: That's right.

GIRL: I know it is. And whoa means no.

GUY: I assumed as much. That's why we separated.

GIRL: Uh huh.

GUY: It's true.

GIRL: Had I not said that, would you've . . .

GUY: Probably not.

GIRL: Probably not?!

GUY: Why would I stop if you didn't speak up?

GIRL: I wasn't into it.

GUY: All right.

GIRL: But that doesn't matter to you.

GUY: It matters.

GIRL: Oh yeah?

GUY: I would want you to enjoy—I would want anyone to enjoy it.

GIRL: Is that why you ignored my body language?

GUY: I thought it was normal.

GIRL: It wasn't.

GUY: My bad.

GIRL: Pick up girls at the bar often?

GUY: . . . It's occurred before.

GIRL: How many of them did you not stop for?

GUY: I've never been in this situation.

GIRL: Yeah, never.

GUY: I haven't!

GIRL: We're done here.

GUY: Are we?

GIRL: I think this needs to end.

    (GUY breaks for the door again.)

GUY: I'm on my way then.

GIRL: Good riddance.

GUY: You want my contact info so you can reach out to me ten years down the road and ruin my life for one awkward night?

GIRL: How. Dare. You.

GUY: I dare.

GIRL: I would like it actually.

GUY: Oh, would you?

GIRL: Yes, because I've never been made to feel like this.

GUY: Neither have I!

GIRL: Go. (*Silence.*) GO.

    (*Silence.*)

GUY: This isn't how I wanted the night to turn out.

GIRL: Want in one hand, crap in the other and . . .

GUY: I'm sorry for not getting consent *throughout* the evening. Thought I had it. But I should've kept . . .

GIRL: Woulda shoulda coulda.

GUY: Yeah . . . (*Sincere.*) Have a good night.

    (*GIRL cackles as he exits. Then begins to cry. Lights dim. Blackout.*)

END OF PLAY

ZOO THEORY

JACOB T. ZACK

Original production
First produced at NJ Repertory Company
October 5, 2019
Directed by: John FitzGibbon

Cast:
JANE: Mary Francina Golden
DIANE: Karen Christie-Ward

CHARACTERS

DIANE, an Octopus.
JANE, a Penguin.

SETTING

The South Pole. The walls are blue, the floor is blue. Blue blocks are scattered around the stage. A cardboard sign downstage center with an arrow pointing upstage that reads "South Pole," an arrow pointing to the right that reads "Amazon and Food Court," and an arrow pointing left that reads "Sahara and Restrooms." A surveillance camera upstage center near the ceiling, pointing directly at the audience, flashing red throughout the play.

• • •

Lights up on the South Pole. Enter DIANE and JANE. DIANE wears an octopus costume, walking awkwardly with several legs dragging on the floor. JANE wears a penguin costume, walking normally.

DIANE: (*Gesturing at the space.*) Here we are.

JANE: Wow.

DIANE: Home sweet home.

JANE: (*Taking it in.*) Not bad.

DIANE: How's the temperature?

JANE: (*Marveling.*) I've never been so cold!

DIANE: Apparently, this is what the South Pole would have looked and felt like.

JANE: Incredible.

DIANE: It's been a while since we've had a Penguin.

JANE: (*Moving around the room.*) And it's spacious!

DIANE: You should have 3–4 ice chunks, an ice wall, a sleeping cave, and a large hammer.

(*They look around the room in unison to ensure that everything is in order.*)

JANE: Looks good to me.

DIANE: To conclude your orientation, I'll need to read the following statement.

(*JANE sits on one of the blocks. DIANE produces a small paper.*)

Welcome to the Zoological Repertory Company, a non-degree conferring unit of the 501(c)3 organization Humans Ontologically Transitioning, or "HOT" for short. As your orientation lead, I'm delighted to welcome you to the most elite stage-acting institute on Earth, which, as far as planets go, is in a state of permanent and irreversible ecological decline. After the last animal species disappeared in 2169, HOT took the initiative to create an acting school that blends dramaturgical theory with zoological practice. Although there are no more animals on Earth, our society is still able to enjoy a "good ole' fashion trip to the zoo," thanks to our dedicated thespians. You will now perform as your assigned animal, "insert animal here." Sorry. Penguin. (*Pause.*) Over the course of your stay, you'll master "Zoo Theory," have some laughs, and most importantly, make lifelong friends in the process. (*Pause; aside.*) That being said, laughter is prohibited and socialization is totally out of the question. (*Continues reading.*) Happy acting and don't forget, break a leg!

JANE: Break a leg?

DIANE: (*Folding up paper.*) It's an old acting phrase. No one really knows what it means. (*Pause.*)

JANE: Is there a bathroom?

DIANE: Most of us are Method Actors.

JANE: So you just—

DIANE: Stanislavski was unambiguous. (*Pause.*)

JANE: Have you been in the company long?

DIANE: (*Sits, crosses legs and arms.*) I started as a Mountain Goat in the Himalaya section, but I really cut my teeth as a Pelican in the Seaside habitat.

JANE: And now you're underwater.

DIANE: 10,000 feet.

JANE: That must be exciting.

DIANE: Octopus has been great for my career.

JANE: I can only imagine.

DIANE: Where did you say you trained again?

JANE: I've had plenty of training. Classes, workshops. Theater. Different cities. Film. Commercials. I've also done some work with John . . .

DIANE: Oh, I know John.

JANE: You do?

DIANE: Isn't he the best?

JANE: We're extremely close.

DIANE: I owe him my career!

JANE: He's been crucial to my development.

DIANE: I've always felt that I could call him for anything, at anytime.

JANE: He's nothing if not reliable.

DIANE: Steady as they come.

JANE: I had dinner with him just last week—

DIANE: He was at my wedding—

JANE: My daughter's communion—

DIANE: My son's bris—

JANE: It's how we named our firstborn. (*Pause.*)

DIANE: I assume you've done research into Penguins?

JANE: Oh, sure.

DIANE: The South Pole is no cakewalk. It's our most popular habitat.

JANE: Acting in the Zoo has been a dream for as long as I can remember.

DIANE: What we do is more than acting! We purvey truth. We explore the unknown. We live life, in a way that is more real than how life . . . is actually lived.

JANE: Any advice for how I can best do . . . that . . . on my first day?

DIANE: For starters, you'll need to work on your waddle.

JANE: My—

DIANE: Waddle, yes. Let's see it.

> (*JANE does a mock Penguin waddle. She circles one of the ice blocks. Afterwards, she sits down.*)

That's good. I really like the choice you made at the end. I found myself wondering, is that how a Penguin would walk?

JANE: Right, and I thought it—

DIANE: And THEN the question is, is that how a Penguin SHOULD walk? (*Pause.*)

JANE: (*Confused.*) Um.

DIANE: (*Moving downstage center, flapping her Octopus arms as she theorizes.*) What you need to understand is that no one in the audience has ever seen a Penguin. Neither have their parents nor their grandparents. They don't care how Penguins walked. They want to see how YOUR Penguin walks.

JANE: So, I should walk like a human?

DIANE: (*Revolted.*) God no. Anything but that.

> (*JANE stands up, takes a few steps waddling as before, and then decides to jump around the block on one leg. JANE sits, gasps, clapping.*)

Now THAT was truth! I did not see that coming. And I guarantee: neither will they.

JANE: The audience won't care if I do . . . my own Penguin?

DIANE: The world had thousands of years to enjoy Penguins. Now it's your turn.

JANE: It's my Penguin.

DIANE: And that's the crux of Zoo Theory: it's your Penguin. And what's best, you never know who might be out in that crowd. Agents used to go Off-Broadway, now they come to the Zoo.

JANE: I don't want to get cage-fright.

DIANE: Being a Penguin is serious. Have you worked on your mating call?

> (*Pause. Then, JANE barks like a dog.*)

Not entirely original, but it should be fine. How does a Penguin show affection?

> (*Pause. JANE spits on the floor.*)

DIANE: (*Considers, and then.*) Could use more distance. But still, very nice. How does a Penguin demonstrate arousal?

> (*Pause. JANE hunches over a block and growls like a rabid animal.*)

Excellent.

JANE: I had no idea there was so much room for biological interpretation.

DIANE: As long as you live your truth, and by your truth I mean the Penguin's truth, and by the Penguin's truth I mean your truth, you'll be great. People will be watching your every move. And we haven't even discussed the Zoo Keepers.

(*They both glance up at the camera.*)

JANE: (*Looking at the camera.*) Will I be able to meet them? I'd love to find out who is behind the whole . . .

DIANE: (*Noticing something on the floor downstage left.*) Hey, it looks like the ice is cracked. Here, come take a look . . .

JANE: What is it? I don't see . . .

(*Once they are downstage left, DIANE pulls JANE down onto the floor. DIANE starts whispering loudly and frantically.*)

DIANE: (*Whispering.*) Will you SHUT UP for a second? If you're lucky, you'll NEVER meet them!

JANE: (*Whispering.*) But what if I have—

DIANE: (*Whispering.*) They're watching us. Always! Be careful. Do what they say. Stay in character. As much as possible. Penguin all the time! Otherwise, something terrible might happen.

JANE: (*Whispering.*) Terrible how?

DIANE: (*Whispering.*) They'll have you relocated.

JANE: (*Whispering.*) A little diversity could be nice . . .

DIANE: (*Whispering.*) Somewhere horrible!

JANE: (*Whispering.*) Such as?

DIANE: (*Whispering.*) The desert section.

JANE: (*Whispering.*) Some like it hot . . . don't they?

DIANE: (*Whispering.*) How'd you like to be a scorpion, baking in the sun?

JANE: (*Whispering.*) I'd never thought about that.

DIANE: (*Whispering.*) Or even worse, they'll have you . . . well, how do I put this . . .

JANE: (*Whispering.*) What?

DIANE: (*Whispering.*) Let's just say they're always expanding the fossil repository. (*Pause.*)

JANE: (*Whispering.*) I see.

DIANE: (*Loudly, standing.*) The ice looks good. Must have been my mistake.

JANE: (*Loudly, standing.*) Don't worry about it.

DIANE: Any other questions?

JANE: Can we socialize with other . . . animals?

DIANE: (*Sighs. Then, "notices" something on the floor downstage right.*) Oh no, another crack! Here, come see . . .

JANE: Where? I don't see . . .

(*Once they are downstage right, DIANE pulls JANE down again.*)

DIANE: (*Whispering.*) Shut up, just SHUT UP! Ok listen. We aren't supposed to, but a few of us get together in the birdcage on weekends.

JANE: (*Whispering.*) The birdcage?

DIANE: (*Whispering.*) Follow the chirping. Come after nightfall. In character!

JANE: (*Whispering.*) Got it.

DIANE: (*Loudly, standing.*) My mistake again. All that algae . . . must be messing with my eyesight!

JANE: (*Loudly, standing.*) No problem!

DIANE: Anything else?

JANE: Are there any opportunities to play other roles?

DIANE: Other roles?

JANE: Obviously I'm committed to Penguin. But I'd love to explore different parts.

DIANE: Most actors would claw their eyes out to get into the South Pole. What could be better?

JANE: I've heard great things about the apes. Apparently, they're so dedicated to their parts that they become . . . almost human.

DIANE: (*Hushed tone.*) That's nothing. Have you heard about . . . Bear?

JANE: (*Hushed tone.*) Bear?

DIANE: (*Hushed tone.*) No one knows his real name. He used to be the director of the company. One day, he decided to demonstrate a Grizzly for the class.

JANE: (*Hushed tone.*) And?

DIANE: (*Hushed tone.*) He's been demonstrating ever since.

JANE: (*Hushed tone.*) No.

DIANE: (*Hushed tone.*) Word is that the Zoo Keepers were so pleased that they gifted him . . . I shouldn't say.

JANE: Tell me.

DIANE: A massage chair.

JANE: Really?

DIANE: He keeps it in his sleeping cave. The neighboring habitats can hear the vibration.

JANE: I'd love a massage chair. Or an espresso machine, or, or . . .

DIANE: You've got a long way to go.

JANE: What's his secret?

DIANE: With every action, you need to ask yourself "what would my character do?"

JANE: Got it. (*Pause.*)

JANE: Before you go, can you help me move some of these blocks?

DIANE: My character probably wouldn't do that.

JANE: I see. (*Pause.*)

DIANE: I actually have to clean the glass in my tank, would you mind—

JANE: Oh, my character definitely wouldn't do that.

DIANE: Very good. (*Pause.*)

JANE: Do you want to stay a while?

DIANE: I want to, obviously. But my character . . . well, I have to be going.

JANE: I understand.

DIANE: (*Walks over to JANE, drapes her many arms on JANE's shoulders.*) You're going to shine. Remember: it's YOUR Penguin. And whatever you do, don't forget: break a leg!

> (*She exits. The lights dim slightly. JANE sits quietly for a moment and then starts to waddle/hop around the room, humming. Finally, she arrives at the hammer.*)

JANE: (*Weighing her options.*) It'd be consistent with my waddle . . . (*She grabs the hammer and hops towards an ice block. To herself:*) It's your Penguin. It's your Penguin. (*Pause.*) Massage chair. (*She props one leg up on an ice block and raises the hammer overhead.*)

> (*Blackout.*)

END OF PLAY

TEN-MINUTE PLAY PRODUCERS

The Actors Studio of Newburyport
TASN Short Play Festival
www.newburyportacting.org
Contact Marc Clopton, info@newburyportacting.org

Acts on the Edge, Santa Monica
mariannesawchuk@hotmail.com

American Globe Theatre Turnip Festival
Gloria Falzer
gfalzer@verizon.net

The Arc Theatre
arciTEXT Ten-Minute Play Festival
https://arctheatrechicago.org
Contact Natalie Sallee: natalie@arctheatrechicago.org

Artistic Home Theatre Co.
Cut to the Chase Festival
Kathy Scambiatterra, Artistic Director:
artistic.director@theartistichome.org

Artists' Exchange
One Act Play Festival
Jessica Chace, Artistic Director, OAPF
jessica.chace@artists-exchange.org
www.artists-exchange.org

The ArtsCenter, Carrboro, North Carolina
Jeri Lynn Schulke, director
theatre@artscenterlive.org https://artscenterlive.org/www.artscenterlive.org
/performance/opportunities

Association for Theatre in Higher Education New Play Development Workshop
Contact Charlene A. Donaghy: charlene@charleneadonaghy.com
http://www.athe.org/displaycommon.cfm?an=1&subarticlenbr=70

Auburn Players Community Theatre Short Play Festival
Contact: Bourke Kennedy, bourkekennedy@gmail.com

The Barn Players
http://www.thebarnplayers.org/

Barrington Stage Company
10X10 New Play Festival
Julianne Boyd is the Artistic Director
jboyd@barringtonstageco.org
www.barringtonstageco.org

Belhaven University, Jackson, Mississippi
One Act Festival
Joseph Frost, Department Chair
theatre@belhaven.edu

Blue Slipper Theatre, Livingston, Montana
Marc Beaudin, Festival Director
blueslipper10fest@gmail.com
www.blueslipper.com

Boston Theater Marathon
Boston Playwrights Theatre
www.bostonplaywrights.org
Kate Snodgrass (ksnodgra@bu.edu)
Plays by New England playwrights only

Boulder Life Festival, Boulder, Colorado
Dawn Bower, Director of Theatrical Program
(dawn@boulderlifefestival.com)
www.boulderlifefestival.com

Box Factory for the Arts
Judith Sokolowski, President
boxfactory@sbcglobal.net
www.boxfactoryforthearts.org

The Brick Theater's "Tiny Theater Festival"
Michael Gardner, Artistic Director
mgardner@bricktheater.com
www.bricktheater.com

Broken Nose Theatre
Benjamin Brownson, Artistic Director
Bechdel Fest
www.brokennosetheatre.com/bechdel-fest-3
ben@brokennosetheatre.com

The Brooklyn Generator
Erin Mallon
brooklyngenerator@outlook.com
https://www.facebook.com/TheBrooklynGenerator/info
https://thetanknyc.org/the-brooklyn-generator

Camino Real Playhouse
www.caminorealplayhouse.org

Chalk Repertory Theatre Flash Festival produced by Chalk Repertory Theatre
Contact person: Ruth McKee
ruthamckee@aol.com
www.chalkrep.com

Chameleon Theatre Circle, Burnsville, MN 55306
www.chameleontheatre.org
jim@chameleontheatre.org

Chagrin Valley Little Theatre
The 10-10 Festival
www.cvlt.org
cvlt@cvlt.org

Changing Scene Theatre Northwest
Pavlina Morris
changingscenenorthwest@hotmail.com

Cherry Picking
http://www.cherrypicking.nyc/
cherrypickingnyc@gmail.com

City Theatre
www.citytheatre.com
Susan Westfall
susan@citytheatre.com

City Theatre of Independence
Annual Playwrights Festival
www.citytheatreofindependence.org

The Collective NY
C10 Play Festival
www.thecollective-ny.org
thecollective9@gmail.com

Colonial Playhouse
Colonial Quickies
www.colonialplayhouse.net
colonialplayhousetheater@40yahoo.com

Company of Angels
1350 San Pablo St, Los Angeles, CA 90033
(213) 489-3703 (main office)
armevan@sbcglobal.net

Core Arts Ensemble
coreartsensemble@gmail.com

Därkhorse Drämatists
www.darkhorsedramatists.com
darkhorsedramatists@gmail.com

Darknight Productions
4 Women Only and 4 Men Only
www.darknightproductions.com

Distilled Theatre Co.
submissions.dtc@gmail.com

Edmonds Driftwood Players
www.driftwoodplayers.com
shortssubmissions@driftwoodplayers.com
tipsproductions@driftwoodplayers.com

The Drilling Company
Hamilton Clancy
drillingcompany@aol.com

Durango Arts Center 10-Minute Play Festival
www.durangoarts.org
Theresa Carson
TenMinutePlayDirector@gmail.com

Eden Prairie Players
www.edenprairieplayers.com

Eastbound Theatre 10-Minute Festival (In the summer: themed.)
Contact Person: Tom Rushen
email: ZenRipple@yahoo.com

East Haddam Stage Company
Contact person: Kandie Carl
email: Kandie@ehsco.org

Emerging Artists Theatre
Fall EATFest
www.emergingartiststheatre.org

En Avant Playwrights
https://www.tapatalk.com/groups/enavantplaywrights/opportunities-10
-minute-other-short-plays-f3/

Ensemble Theatre of Chattanooga Short Attention Span Theatre Festival
Contact Person: Garry Posey (Artistic Director)
garryposey@gmail.com
www.ensembletheatreofchattanooga.com

Fell's Point Corner Theatre 10 x 10 Festival
Contact Person: Richard Dean Stover (rick@fpct.org)
www.fpct.org

Fem Noire (plays by New England women playwrights)
Image Theater
www.imagetheater.com
imagetheaterlowell@gmail.com

Fine Arts Association
Annual One Act Festival-Hot from the Oven Smorgasbord
ahedger@fineartsassociation.org

Firehouse Center for the Arts, Newburyport, Massachusetts
New Works Festival
Kimm Wilkinson, Director
www.firehouse.org
Limited to New England playwrights

Flush Ink Productions
Asphalt Jungle Shorts Festival
www.flushink.net/AJS.html

The Fringe of Marin Festival
Contact Person: Annette Lust
email: jeanlust@aol.com

Fury Theatre
katie@furytheare.org
Fusion Theatre Co.
http://www.fusionabq.org
info@fusionabq.org

Future Ten
info@futuretenant.org

Gallery Players
Annual Black Box Festival
info@galleryplayers.com

Gaslight Theatre
www.gaslight-theatre.org
gaslighttheatre@gmail.com

GI60
Steve Ansell
screammedia@yahoo.com

The Gift Theatre
TEN Festival
Contact: Michael Patrick Thornton
www.thegifttheatre.org

Good Works Theatre Festival
Good Acting Studio
www.goodactingstudio.com

The Greenhouse Ensemble
Ten-Minute Play Soiree
www.greenhouseensemble.com

Heartland Theatre Company
Themed Ten-Minute Play Festival Every Year
Contact Person: Mike Dobbins (Artistic Director)
boxoffice@heartlandtheatre.org
www.heartlandtheatre.org

Hella Fresh Fish
freshfish2submit@gmail.com

The Hovey Players, Waltham, Massachusetts
Hovey Summer Shorts
www.hoveyplayers.com

Image Theatre
Naughty Shorts
jbisantz@comcast.net

Island Theatre Ten-Minute Play Festival
www.islandtheatre.org

Ixion Ensemble, Lansing, Michigan
Jeff Croff, Artistic Director
Ixionensemble@gmail.com

Kings Theatre
www.kingstheatre.ca

Lakeshore Players
https://www.lakeshoreplayers.org
ATTN: Joan Elwell
office@lakeshoreplayers.org

Lee Street Theatre, Salisbury, North Carolina (themed)
Original 10-Minute Play Festival
Justin Dionne, managing artistic director
info@leestreet.org
www.leestreet.org

Little Black Dress Ink
ATTN: Tiffany Antone.
Email: info@LittleBlackDressINK.org
www.LittleBlackDressINK.org

Little Fish Theatre Co.
Pick of the Vine Festival
holly@littlefishtheatre.org www.littlefishtheatre.org

Live Girls Theatre
submissions@lgtheater.org

Luna Stage
New Moon Short Play Festival
submissions@lunastage.org.
www.lunastage.org

MadLab Theatre
Theatre Roulette
Andy Batt (andy@madlab.net)
www.madlab.net

Magnolia Arts Center, Greenville, North Carolina
Ten-Minute Play Contest
info@magnoliaartscenter.com
www.magnoliaartscenter.com
Fee charged

Manhattan Repertory Theatre, New York, New York
Ken Wolf
manhattanrep@yahoo.com
www.manhattanrep.com

McLean Drama Company
www.mcleandramacompany.org
Rachel Bail (rachbail@yahoo.com)

Miami 1-Acts Festival (two sessions—Winter [December] and Summer [July])
Contact: Steven A. Chambers, Literary Manager (schambers@new-theatre.org)
Ricky J. Martinez, Artistic Director (rjmartinez@new-theatre.org)
www.new-theatre.org
Submission Requirements: No more than 10–15 pages in length; subject is not specific, though plays can reflect life in South Florida and the tropics and the rich culture therein. Area playwrights are encouraged to submit, though the festival is open to national participation. Deadline for the Winter Session is October 15 of each year; deadline for the Summer Session is May 1 of each year.

Milburn Stone Theatre One Act Festival
www.milburnstone.org

Mildred's Umbrella Theater Company
Museum of Dysfunction Festival
www.mildredsumbrella.com
info@mildredsumbrella.com

Mill 6 Collaborative
John Edward O'Brien, Artistic Director
mill6theatre@gmail.com

Napa Valley Players
8 × 10: A Festival of 10-Minute Plays
www. http://www.valley-players.com/

Newburgh Free Academy
tsandler@necsd.net

The New American Theatre
www.newamericantheatre.com
Play Submissions: JoeBays44@earthlink.net

New Jersey Rep
Theatre Brut Festival
Their yearly Theatre Brut Festival is organized around a specified theme.
njrep@njrep.org

New Urban Theatre Laboratory
5 & Dime
Jackie Davis, Artistic Director:
jackie.newurbantheatrelab@gmail.com

New Voices Original Short Play Festival
Kurtis Donnelly (kurtis@gvtheatre.org)

NFA New Play Festival
Newburgh Free Academy
201 Fullerton Ave, Newburgh, NY 12550
Terry Sandler: terrysandle@hotmail.com
(May not accept electronic submissions.)

North Park Playwright Festival
New short plays (no more than 15 pages, less is fine)
Submissions via mail to:
North Park Vaudeville and Candy Shoppe
2031 El Cajon Blvd.
San Diego, CA 92104

Attn: Summer Golden, Artistic Director.
www.northparkvaudeville.com

Northport One-Act Play Festival
Jo Ann Katz (joannkatz@gmail.com)
www.northportarts.org

The Now Collective
Sean McGrath
Sean@nowcollective@gmail.com

NYC Playwrights
https://www.nycplaywrights.org/search/label/10-minute%20plays

Northwest 10 Festival of Ten-Minute Plays
Sponsored by Oregon Contemporary Theatre
https://www.octheatre.org/home
Email: NW10Festival@gmail.com

Nylon Fusion Theatre Company
nylonsubmissions@gmail.com
https://www.nylonfusion.org/

Onion Man Productions Summer Harvest
onionmanproductions@gmail.com

Open Tent Theatre Co.
Ourglass 24 Hour Play Festival
opententtheater@gmail.com

Otherworld Theatre
Paragon Festival: Sci-fi and fantasy plays
Elliott Sowards, literary manager of Otherworld Theatre and curator of the
Paragon Play Festival, elliott@otherworldtheatre.org
www.otherworldtheatre.org

Over Our Head Players, Racine, Wisconsin
www.overourheadplayers.org/oohp15

Pan Theater, Oakland, California
Anything Can Happen Festival
David Alger, pantheater@comcast.net
http://www.pantheater.com

Pandora Theatre, Houston, Texas
Vox Feminina
Melissa Mumper, Artistic Director
pandoratheatre@sbcglobal.net

Paw Paw Village Players One Act Festival
www.ppvp.org

Pegasus Theater Company (in Sonoma County, north of San Francisco)
Tapas Short Plays Festival
www.pegasustheater.comm
Contact: Lois Pearlman lois5@sonic.net

Philadelphia Theatre Company
PTC@Play New Work Festival
Contact: Jill Harrison
jillian.harrison@gmail.com
www.philadelphiatheatrecompany.org

PianoFight Productions, L.A.
ShortLivedLA@gmail.com

Piney Fork Press Theater Play Festival
Johnny Culver, submissions@pineyforkpress.com
www.pineyforkpress.com

The Playgroup LLC
Boca Raton, Florida
theplaygroupllc@gmail.com
www.theplaygroupllc.com

Playhouse Creatures
Page to Stage
newplays@playhousecreatures.org

Play on Words Productions
playonwordsproductions@gmail.com
Megan Kosmoski, Producing Artist Director

Playpalooza
Backstage at SPTC (Santa Paula Theatre Co.)
John McKinley, Artistic Director
sptcbackstage@gmail.com

Playwrights' Arena
Flash Theater LA
Contact person: Jon Lawrence Rivera
jonlawrencerivera@gmail.com
www.playwrightsarena.org

Playwrights' Round Table, Orlando, Florida
Summer Shorts
Chuck Dent charlesrdent@hotmail.com
www.theprt.com

Playwrights Studio Theater
5210 W. Wisconsin Ave.
Milwaukee, WI 53208
Attn: Michael Neville, Artistic Dir.

Renegade Theatre Festival
http://www.renegadetheatrefestival.org/

Rotate Theatre
Chicago Indie Boots Festival
www.indieboots.org

Salem Theatre Co.
Moments of Play
New England playwrights only.
mop@salemtheatre.com

Santa Cruz Actors' Theatre
Eight Tens at Eight
Wilma Chandler, Artistic Director
ronziob@email.com
http://www.sccat.org

The Secret Theatre (Midsummer Night Festival), Queens, New York
Odalis Hernandez, odalis.hernandez@gmail.com
www.secrettheatre.com/

She Speaks, Kitchener, Ontario
Paddy Gillard-Bentley (paddy@skyedragon.com)
Women playwrights

Shelterbelt Theatre, Omaha, Nebraska
From Shelterbelt with Love
McClain Smouse, associate-artistic@shelterbelt.org
submissions@shelterbelt.org
www.shelterbelt.org

Shepparton Theatre Arts Group
"Ten in 10" is a performance of ten plays each running for ten minutes every year.
info@stagtheatre.com
www.stagtheatre.com

Short+Sweet
Literary Manager, Pete Malicki
Pete@shortandsweet.org
http://www.shortandsweet.org/shortsweet-theatre/submit-script

Silver Spring Stage, Silver Spring, Maryland
Jacy D'Aiutolo
oneacts2012.ssstage@gmail.com
www.ssstage.org

Sixth Street Theatre
Snowdance Ten-Minute Comedy Festival
Rich Smith
Snowdance318@gmail.com

Source Festival
jenny@culturaldc.org

Southern Rep Theatre
6×6
Aimee Hayes (literary@southernrep.com)
www.southernrep.com/

Stage Door Productions
Original One-Act Play Festival
www.stagedoorproductions.org

Stage Door Repertory Theatre
www.stagedoorrep.org

Stage Q
www.stageq.com

Stillwater Short Play Festival
Town and Gown Theatre (Stillwater, Oklahoma)
Debbie Sutton (producer)
snobiz123@aol.com

Stonington Players
HVPanciera@aol.com
Stratton Players
Stratton Summer Shorts
President: Rachel D'onfro
www.strattonplayers.com
info@strattonplayers.com

Subversive Theatre Collective
Kurt Schneiderman, Artistic Director
www.subversivetheatre.org
info@subversivetheatre.org

Ten Tuckey Festival
doug@thebardstown.com

The Theatre Lab
733 8th St., NW
Washington, DC 20001
https://www.theatrelab.org/
Contact: Buzz Mauro (buzz@theatrelab.org, 202-824-0449)

Theatre Odyssey
Sarasota, Florida
Tom Aposporos Vice President
www.theatreodyssey.org

Theatre One Productions
theatreoneproductions@yahoo.com

Theatre Out, Santa Ana, California
David Carnevale david@theatreout.com
LGBT plays

Theatre Oxford 10-Minute Play Contest
http://www.theatreoxford.com
Alice Walker
10minuteplays@gmail.com

Theatre Roulette Play Festival
Madlab Theatre Co.
andyb@mablab.net

Theatre Three
www.theatrethree.com
Jeffrey Sanzel (jeffrey@theatrethree.com)

Theatre Westminster
Ten Minute New (And Nearly New) Play Festival
ATTN: Terry Dana Jachimiak II
jachimtd@westminster.edu

Theatre Works Ten-Minute Play Festival
https://theatreworks.us/playfestival-event.php

Those Women Productions
www.thosewomenproductions.com

TouchMe Philly Productions
www.touchmephilly.wordpress.com
touchmephilly@gmail.com

Towne Street Theatre Ten-Minute Play Festival
info@townestreet.org

Underground Railway Theatre
https://www.centralsquaretheater.org/about/underground-railway-theater/
Debra Wise, Artistic Director (debra@undergroundrailwaytheatre.org)

Unrenovated Play Festival
unrenovatedplayfest@gmail.com

Walking Fish Theatre
freshfish2submit@gmail.com

Weathervane Playhouse
8 X 10 Theatrefest
info@weathervaneplayhouse.com

Wide Eyed Productions
www.wideeyedproductions.com
playsubmissions@wideeyedproductions.com

Winston-Salem Writers
Annual 10 Minute Play Contest
www.wswriters.org
info@wswriters.org

Write Act Repertory
www.writeactrep.org
John Lant (j316tlc@pacbell.net)

1